SIR HALLEY STEWART TRUST: PUBLICATIONS

Volume 9

THEY ALL COME OUT

THEY ALL COME OUT

G. M. F. BISHOP

Routledge
Taylor & Francis Group

LONDON AND NEW YORK

First published in 1965 by George Allen & Unwin Ltd.

This edition first published in 2025
by Routledge
4 Park Square, Milton Park, Abingdon, Oxon OX14 4RN

and by Routledge
605 Third Avenue, New York, NY 10158

Routledge is an imprint of the Taylor & Francis Group, an informa business

British Library Cataloguing in Publication Data
A catalogue record for this book is available from the British Library

ISBN: 978-1-032-88962-7 (Set)
ISBN: 978-1-032-88633-6 (Volume 9) (hbk)
ISBN: 978-1-032-88640-4 (Volume 9) (pbk)
ISBN: 978-1-003-53882-0 (Volume 9) (ebk)

DOI: 10.4324/9781003538820

Publisher's Note
The publisher has gone to great lengths to ensure the quality of this reprint but points out that some imperfections in the original copies may be apparent.

Disclaimer
The publisher has made every effort to trace copyright holders and would welcome correspondence from those they have been unable to trace.

This book is a re-issue originally published in 1965. The language used and views portrayed are a reflection of its era and no offence is meant by the Publishers to any reader by this re-publication.

THEY ALL COME OUT

BY

G. M. F. BISHOP

PUBLISHED FOR
THE SIR HALLEY STEWART TRUST

GEORGE ALLEN & UNWIN LTD
LONDON

FIRST PUBLISHED IN 1965

PRINTED IN GREAT BRITAIN
in 11 *point Baskerville type*
BY UNWIN BROTHERS LTD
WOKING AND LONDON

To my husband
for
his unfailing support

All opinions expressed in this book are the author's.
All illustrations given are of actual cases, but great care has been taken to conceal identities by the use of different names and places.

CONTENTS

		page
GLOSSARY		10
1.	*The Prison*	15
2.	*What is a Prisoner Like?*	25
3.	*After-Care Begins*	42
4.	*Pre-Release*	68
5.	*Coming Out*	82
6.	*An Experiment in After-Care*	103
7.	*It Could be Different*	120
8.	*Not Only Coming Out*	137

GLOSSARY

Baron	One who organizes a trade in tobacco
Bird	The prison sentence A girl
Blow	To run away, disappear
Choky	Punishment cells in a prison
Con man	Confidence trickster
Doing time	Doing a prison sentence
Escort	A prison officer accompanying a prisoner
Fence	One who gets rid of stolen goods
Grape-vine	The network by which news gets round a prison
'Job'	A crime
Lag	Man who has served years in prison
Nick	Slang for prison
Nicked	Put on punishment
Over the wall	Method of escaping
Peter	Cell
Recidivist	One who returns to prison many times
Remission	Proportion of sentence not served if behaviour is good
Screw	Prison officer
Screwing	House breaking
Snout	Tobacco
Tailor made	Cigarettes not hand made
Time	The sentence
To grass	To tell tales to authorities
Up the steps	Up the steps to the dock for trial

INTRODUCTION

The prison population of this country has risen alarmingly during this century, and now exceeds 24,000, of which only 696 are women. Since 98 per cent of all cases are dealt with in magistrates' courts each year, and these include many sentences for short term imprisonment varying from one to six months, the total number of discharges from prisons all over the country is greatly in excess of the numbers serving sentences at any one time.

This means that every year a far larger number of prisoners are released back into society than many people realise. The most recent figures show that discharges were 50,374 men and 2,659 women in the last complete year. This figure includes those discharged on being sentenced to other forms of treatment. The average cost of keeping a prisoner during the same year was £501 7s 9d, excluding the cost of new prison buildings. In addition to this cost there are large numbers of married men with families which have to be supported by National Assistance and various social services, which again falls on the tax-payer.

In order to deal effectively with this whole problem it must also be borne in mind that Courts must be run, and a Police Force maintained sufficient to provide an adequate service. On the financial side alone it is essential that more must be done to reduce crime, and particularly to reduce the numbers of men and women reconvicted and sent back to prison. It is in the interest of everybody, as well as of the prisoners themselves, that more efforts are made through research and experiment to reduce this vast problem to reasonable proportions, and that new ways and means of rehabilitating ex-prisoners must be brought into force.

Some responsibility for after-care rests inevitably on

members of the public who, by their attitude to the discharged prisoner, their willingness to accept back into society those who have offended against the laws of the country, can influence the attitude of the ex-criminal towards a new way of life.

It is with such a need in view that this book has been written, for there are countless people of good will outside the prison service who, through no fault of their own, are unaware of the contribution they could make to assist the statutory and voluntary organisations already doing so much to rehabilitate men and women released from prison.

In order to help it is necessary to understand something of the problems and difficulties a prisoner has to face when he is once more free.

Much is being done to provide new prisons, more work for prisoners, better conditions and training in various trades and occupations. New laws are passed and the whole system of the administration of Justice is continually under review. It remains a fact that the rehabilitation of human beings cannot be achieved by these means alone. It is not only educational opportunities, and most certainly not charity, that can bring about the change in a man's outlook and way of life. It is the attitude of acceptance and friendship accorded by ordinary men and women with whom he comes in contact on release, and during his sentence, that in the long run will determine his future.

The man walking down the street, the woman in the bus queue, or someone sitting at the next table in the café may be an ex-prisoner. The years of absence from society, causing a limited outlook, make him more than ordinarily conscious of the attitude of those who speak to him or ignore him. He may be wondering if it would be worth while to go straight, and quite a small thing may tip the balance in the right or wrong direction.

Ex-prisoners need work, accommodation and some-times clothing to supplement the bare necessities with which they are provided. Material needs such as these can be, and are being, provided, but the far greater need is acceptance. They have been out of circulation for periods of months or years and have lived in a very small world in which they have acquired different standards of behaviour—different values. During their imprisonment they have not had to use up energy in maintaining them-selves and their families, so that for long sentence men some of the ability to make decisions has gone. Money values have become confused, and pride in the pursuit of any chosen occupation or accomplishment has often been lost, if it ever existed.

A difficult stage lies between the man who leaves the prison gate at 8 o'clock one morning and the day when he will be able to assume all his responsibilities as a citizen of the free world.

It is the intention of this book to look at the problem in four parts. First, the prison—a territory unknown to the vast majority of free people; secondly, the prisoner himself, his personality and needs; thirdly, it is necessary to look at the help already available, and lastly some experiments and a possible new form of after-care which might do much to reduce the large numbers of men who now fail to keep clear of crime and are returned to custody through inadequacy, immaturity, or inability to fit back into ordinary society.

1

THE PRISON

It has been rightly said that after-care begins, or should begin, the day a man enters prison. It is necessary, therefore, to begin with the prison itself, and what it is like from the prisoner's point of view.

To most people, the forbidding walls which confine the local gaol are their only real picture of prison, and the occasional distant view of a party of men working outside, closely watched by an officer in uniform, may give a fleeting glimpse of prisoners themselves.

Dartmoor, the very name of which conjures up all kinds of pictures in the minds of ordinary people, still continues to provide an unfortunate attraction for tourists. People on bus parties in that area are shown the famous prison as one of the sights, and much embarrassment is caused by other tourists and car parties parked in the neighbourhood who stare with obvious curiosity at men who can be seen in the near-by fields or walking across the road to the quarry.

Most prisons in our country were built more than a hundred years ago. At that time they were greatly in advance of anything else that had preceded them. There is the high surrounding wall with the only entrance a great studded door in which sometimes a smaller door is set for the admission of one man at a time. Somewhere about eye level is a tiny judas window so that an officer can look out and inspect a new arrival before opening the gate. Within is a space big enough to take a large car or small bus or van before another gate bars the way to the inside.

Each side of this small courtyard are buildings where there is always an officer on duty, a room where keys and passes are kept and telephones connected with various parts of the prison. Occasionally there is a visiting room and waiting room for prisoners' families so that they do not have to enter the main prison.

Beyond the second gate is the area on which the main buildings of the prison are built, and nowadays this is partly laid out as a garden to off-set the bleakness of the walls and ugly barred windows. The pattern that was used so widely when these particular prisons were built is a star structure with three or four wings leading out from a central hall. The idea was that supervision would be easier in that way because an officer in the central part could command the wings and see all that was going on. The floors were of stone and each wing resembled a narrow, dreary street with the doors down either side opening into the cells. Until recently, these 'streets' were painted in dark, drab colours and the effect was over-poweringly ugly and depressing. Much has been done lately to introduce colour in decorating, and often skylight windows have been introduced to help alleviate the poor lighting of the old days.

Cells themselves are still small narrow rooms in which a high barred window is opposite the door, the rest of the walls being quite plain. In each door is another judas window through which an officer can look when making his rounds in the evening. The average size of a normal cell is 13 feet long, 7 feet wide, and 9 feet high. In the new prisons the cell is smaller, the proportions are different, and the general intention is to make it impossible to have three in a cell.

One chair and a small shelf or table forms the place

where the inmate must eat his meals, another shelf or shelves will accommodate his few possessions and library books, also his photographs of his wife and family. These, for reasons of space, are usually rationed except in the case of men and women serving very long sentences.

The bed is along one side, and is hard, with a mattress made of a coir-filled tick. Every so often this has to be taken out, picked over and separated where it has become lumpy. During the day blankets and other bed clothes are arranged in neat piles on the bed itself, according to the regulations in each prison. There is also a washing bowl, mug and toothbrush, and the inevitable chamber pot with lid, for use by the inmate during the long hours after he is locked in the cell. The window, set high, has eight or ten small panes, one of which is made to open.

Also on each cell landing is a recess where the sanitary arrangements are contained and above each landing is another similar one, sometimes as many as five landings. The dreary effect is not helped by a stout wire netting stretched across the first floor preventing accidents or deliberate attempts to throw anything from above. The floors are connected by iron staircases, either spiral or straight, leading from one floor to another. Windows to light the main hall are set high in the wall at the end of the wing.

Often along the ground floor there are tables and chairs used for certain prisoners to eat their meals in association with other men and in the prisons for younger prisoners some space may be utilized for a small billiard table or table tennis.

Outside the sleeping quarters there are many other buildings within the wall. There is the administrative block where the offices of the Governor, the Deputy Governor, Welfare Officer and others can be found, and there are the workshops, reception wing and clothing

B

store, kitchen, laundry and hospital wing. There is always a chapel and in the smaller prisons this may have to be used also as a meeting place for film shows and concerts, but in the large ones can sometimes be kept entirely for the use for which it was designed. A smaller Roman Catholic chapel is usually found and Free Church prisoners share the main Anglican Chapel for their services. Apart from the buildings there are parts of the area set aside for recreation and exercise, but this is often extremely limited.

Cells were designed for one man only, but such is the overcrowding at present that thousands of men in local prisons are sharing three in a cell, and the other buildings within the walls are strained to capacity.

New prisons are being built and new designs have been found which will gradually replace these century-old establishments, but in the meantime they must continue to be used.

Such prisons are built for security, and are the ones which most readily come to mind when the public thinks about them, but there are in addition a number of open prisons which resemble army camps, as indeed many of them were during the war. In these places prisoners who have earned the right to be tried in open conditions are given the opportunity of serving part of their sentence in this way. It is a challenge to a man or woman to see if they can accept the kind of life such prisons provide and there is opportunity of outside work sometimes on farms belonging to the prison itself, or often in small parties on other farms, or government work in the area. Undoubtedly this is a move in the right direction, because in open conditions much more responsibility is placed on the prisoner and he is therefore learning some independence and control which stands him in good stead after release.

Meals are taken in large dining rooms, and recreation is provided by playing fields. The life is much like that of a camp except for the fact that a man or woman is still a prisoner and is not free to leave.

People outside are quite inconsistent in their views about prisons. Whenever it is announced that a new prison is to be built there is always an outcry from the public who live in the vicinity. All kinds of stories fly about and certain well-known rumours begin to take shape.

'Have you heard about the new prison?'

'Isn't it awful?'

'We shall be murdered in our beds!'

'It won't be safe to go out at nights.'

'They never ought to allow it!'

Conversely there has been quite an outcry at the suggestion that the prison at Dartmoor should be closed, and the prisoners sent elsewhere. It would seem that the people of Princetown love their prison and would be sad to see it go, though maybe the sight-seeers have accounted for this by bringing trade, as the prison has also meant work for those who live nearby.

It is more than apparent that something drastic must be done to counter the increasing numbers of people committed to prison, but in the meantime many new buildings must still be put up.

Everyone agrees that in our civilisation there need to be places where men and women can be detained, and where they can be deprived of their liberty in order to protect the public from their criminal actions.

Life in prison follows a fairly close pattern in most of the closed institutions. The day begins early, the bell ringing at 6.30 a.m. and by seven o'clock cell doors are opened for the process of 'slopping out', which means emptying chambers. This particular office, though greatly improved since the more hygienic sanitary recesses have been built, is still one of the horrors of prison life. Some may feel that the style of included toilets in the cells of United States prisons and of some on the Continent is a far better way and could well be adopted here. One criticism against it is that there is the possibility of drain stoppage through the misuse of toilets, but other countries where such cell equipment is used, have not found this an insuperable barrier to better facilities.

At 7.15 breakfast is served in the cell, and at 7.55 follows a period of exercise in the open air. At one time prisoners walked round and round in single file, in a circle, forbidden to speak, but nowadays they walk about in twos and threes talking and smoking an odd cigarette from their small ration.

At 8.30 a.m. work begins. This may be in one of the workshops of the prison, or in the laundry, kitchen or garden, or the cleaning and maintenance of the main buildings.

Twelve-fifteen p.m. is lunch time, again in cells for many, or in association with other prisoners. Lunch is followed by half an hour of exercise, and another period of work. Tea is at 5.15 and this is a cooked meal. After tea some men remain in their cells for the rest of the evening, but many elect to join the voluntary educational classes, which are run in the prison, usually from 6.30–7.30 p.m. In the last few years opportunities such as this have been provided and many men have been able to pursue their interests and hobbies. Some have studied subjects which will be useful to them on release, others making toys and handicrafts which they may later buy for their families. Much beautiful work has been done in these groups, and it is an opportunity for those skilled in painting or other handicrafts or music to do some really artistic work. These classes are arranged with the help of the local education committees and with teachers supplied by them.

It has been found in many prisons that classes are also needed in basic English, as certain prisoners are illiterate.

It is important that all evening classes should be voluntary but this also creates some problems. In prison there are few ways in which anyone can exercise the power of choice, and therefore it is a very important right to be able to say 'No'. Some have missed the benefits that might have been theirs because they have exercised this right to the detriment of their future progress. Men and women serving short sentences of three months and under are not eligible for classes and so they often derive no benefit educationally from their imprisonment.

Officially there is always choice in the matter of work and of evening classes, but this does not always mean that a man can do what he chooses. Some classes and workshops are more popular than others, and often in practice it happens that a man has to wait many months before he can get into the group he has chosen, and some never manage it. In long-term prisons it is likely that a prisoner will eventually achieve this ambition to work or study as he wishes.

Courses in brick-laying, painting and decorating, engineering, motor-mechanics, tailoring and carpentry, to mention only a few of the possible choices, are available in different prisons, and examinations through the City and Guilds can be taken. One day it is hoped that such courses will enable men and women to start at a better level in industry on their release, but this is not so at present.

In open prisons, where the proportion of 'star' prisoners, the name for men and women serving their first sentence, is high, there are sports and playing fields. Matches are sometimes played against outside teams, the only difference being that they are usually played on the prison ground. Opportunities for drama and musical appreciation are provided in a number of prisons, and often people who have never learned to express themselves are able to do this through the medium of music and painting.

Prison hospitals are quite small as a rule. Only certain of the larger prisons have anything similar to an outside hospital. Minor illnesses can easily be dealt with by visiting doctors and if there is need for a major operation or an emergency the nearest general hospital can be used. Dental treatment is also given in prison by visiting dentists.

Church attendance was at one time compulsory, but now some freedom is given in that a man or woman can opt out of attending any service at all. If a particular denomination is chosen then the prisoner wishes to change, permission must be sought from the two chaplains and the Visiting Committee.

All prisons have either Visiting Committees or Boards of Visitors. These men and women are recruited from the area in which a prison is situated. In the case of the former, appointments of local justices are made by Petty Sessional Division and Quarter Sessions and of Benches of local magistrates. Boards of Visitors are appointed by the Secretary of State.

These men and women have certain statutory duties in supervision of all aspects of their prisons, and also act in a disciplinary capacity in certain matters and in the hearing of applications from the prisoners.

The responsibility of such work is obvious. Most prisons are closed communities with few outside contacts, and these men and women are therefore amongst the few people with regular access. Much good is done where Visiting committees and Boards of Visitors take a real interest in their prisons. Inmates have often said how much they have appreciated the additional concern shown by

enlightened Boards where members have not only carried
out the minimum requirements, but have expressed their
interest by attendance at concerts, sports events and other
special occasions connected with the Institutions. In the
old days men only served on Boards of men's prisons,
and women for their own sex, but today in all progressive
prisons men and women serve on these committees bringing their joint experience and knowledge to help in the
better administration of prisons in general.

At the head of each prison is the Governor and a
Deputy Governor who can take charge in his absence.
Some of the larger prisons have also one or more Assistant
Governors. These men are specially selected and trained
to have a good understanding of the whole prison system
and of prisoners themselves. From their ranks are recruited many of the Governors, although it is also possible
for any officer to work his way up to the top through the
ordinary ranks of the service.

In this very brief account of prisons and the type of life
within, mention must be made of the improvements that
are continually being introduced.

The object of a prison sentence, which at one time was
merely punitive and intended to degrade the prisoner as
much as possible, has now changed in that the idea is to
rehabilitate as far as can be done within the security needs.

Rehabilitation is always extremely difficult in captivity,
but steps have been taken and much has been done to
achieve this. Some of these steps will come better under
the heading of pre-release, and will be mentioned in a
later chapter, but here let it be said that the public need
to alter some widely expressed views about new schemes.

People often say 'Prison is a piece of cake these days.
Everything is done for the men's comfort—I don't know
what the world is coming to.' Sometimes a remark has
been made that 'Prison is so easy people try to get in

these days!' These and similar views show that those who express themselves in that way have little imagination and practically no knowledge of what prison means. Let no one think that because certain necessary improvements have come about, that colour and flower gardens have appeared, and a more humane approach is now made to the problems, prison has ceased to be the greatest punishment that can be inflicted, for what is life worth without liberty?

To deprive a human being of freedom, to direct his life so that he is told when to get up, to work, to eat, what to wear, when to wash, and force him even to ask permission to go to the toilet, is a punishment that strikes at the very heart of a man and takes away self-respect. That this was once done in surroundings so dreary and depressing that prisoners saw nothing that was beautiful, nothing that could uplift the spirit, was only to aggravate the bitterness and anti-social feeling that confinement engenders. Although people are unlikely to be in a position to do away with all forms of prison sentences, at least they can strive to improve the conditions in which such sentences are served, so that ultimately these improvements may have some small influence on the outlook of those who have to live in them.

Material influences are important, and play their part in the general effect of the sentence, but by far the most important influences are those which come from contact with people, and it will be necessary to look at the people in the prison service and others who meet or work with the prisoners. First it would be appropriate to look at the prisoners themselves and try to clear away some all-too-prevalent ideas about them which are so often and so carelessly expressed by ill-informed people.

2

WHAT IS A PRISONER LIKE?

The fact that such a question can be asked is a very good reason for writing something about the people who continue to fill our already over-crowded prisons.

There is always great curiosity about prisoners, and from many remarks that have been made to me I know that there is a widely spread idea that prisoners look different from ordinary people. There may be those members of the public who live so close to a prison that they have ceased to regard it as anything unusual, but there are always people who stare and hope to get a glimpse of some famous criminal whose picture has appeared in the national newspapers at the time of the trial.

Naturally steps are taken to prevent this sort of thing, and great restrictions are of necessity placed in the regulations to prevent people with no real reason for their presence seeing the inside of a prison. Possibly because so much of prison life is a mystery, it has given rise to a morbid curiosity from which has grown the tale of the typical criminal features, the unusual ears, and rumours have spread about the depraved and ugly countenances that might be expected within the high walls.

One day I had been making an official visit as speaker to an organisation of women, when I was asked in all seriousness, 'What does a prisoner look like? Are they really so dreadful-looking?'

Such questions show that a great deal more must be

known about prisons and prisoners before people can take a proper and balanced view of the whole subject.

In recent years a number of books have been published, written by ex-prisoners, social workers, prison officers and the Press. Some are excellent and give a true picture of prison life in its various facets, but generally it is not permitted to publish pictures of prisoners, for obvious reasons. Once a man or woman leave gaol it is necessary for them to get a fresh start and to do this they must not be recognised as ex-prisoners. Good television programmes have been shown describing life inside but the man or woman interviewed is usually sitting with the face turned away from the camera, so it may well be that this has given rise to so many curious ideas about the appearance of prisoners.

I know a great many prisoners, and I am quite convinced there is no criminal type. I have known a great many ex-prisoners and never to my knowledge was any such man or woman noticeable in any way, nor had they a depraved appearance which would have made it easy for them to be detected. People who follow most closely the general type that outsiders describe as 'criminal' are often the most respected members of society and have certainly never seen the inside of a prison!

A story illustrating this point may well be included here.

Many years ago an elderly lady of shy and retiring disposition was kind enough to offer voluntary help in some social work in our city. The club was situated in a rather dark street, and a walk of some three hundred yards along a dark pavement led to the nearest bus stop.

This lady had read tales of assault and violence particularly directed towards elderly females. She was nervous and looked round the club at closing time to find someone really kind and respectable to accompany her down the road. Seeing a man whom she had often served and liked very much, she asked him if he would see her to the bus stop, explaining her fears apologetically, and he immediately offered to escort her. Thankfully she took his arm and was duly seen off quite safely. Little did she know that she had picked an ex-prisoner who had served a twelve-year sentence for murder!

Naturally there are some books which, although what is written may have been true as regards certain unfortunate incidents and practices, give a distorted picture and have been 'written up' in order to shock and horrify. Undoubtedly it is right and proper that people should know if things are not right, but it is grossly unfair that the whole prison system should be damned by exaggerating certain points and saying nothing of what is good and worth while. As in any closed community, be it a school, a ship, a hospital or any place where a number of human beings live in a restricted area for months or years, there are bound to be unfortunate incidents at times, and extremely difficult people. These do not mean that the whole system is bad from beginning to end, nor that all the people inside are inhuman monsters. Unfortunate incidents are the exception rather than the rule.

To gain a true picture of the main factors in the make-up of a prisoner, it may be helpful to compare him with ordinary people in a difficult situation.

Imagine a roomful of men and women shut away suddenly from society for a year. Issue them with uniform, fix the times of their meals, sleeping hours and exercise. Make out a timetable to govern their days and set over them officers in uniform to watch that the rules and regulations are carried out to the letter.

What would you find?

There would be the people who were so miserable and depressed at the separation from home and loved ones, that it would be hard to raise them from the apathy into which they had sunk. Some would be so angry at their imprisonment that they would become truculent and aggressive to the officers in charge. Others would attempt to escape, whilst those who accepted the situation and were not too bored and apathetic to use their imagination would devise ways and means of improving their lot by skilful and cunning methods of obtaining more than their fair share of such small luxuries as they could find.

Young and active men and women, deprived of the normal outlets for sexual relationships in marriage, might manage to sublimate their natural desires, but others less controlled might be tempted to provide themselves with something of a homosexual nature if through it they could acquire some affection or some release from strain.

Gossip would be rife. The fact that their world had suddenly become so small and shut in would over-emphasise the importance of all its aspects, and so the focal points of interest would tend to become the people in authority, and any attributes or indiscretions would be magnified beyond all reason.

All effects of the unnatural life would not be bad. There would be the kindnesses shown, appreciation of little thoughtful actions and visits or letters from home would mean more than anyone outside could believe. Even in cases where a husband and wife had not enjoyed perfect companionship and loving understanding before, a new relationship would grow where the need of the imprisoned one might be greater than the generosity of the other.

So far we have imagined a roomful of ordinary people suddenly placed in custody. We have pictured just a few of the many and varied ways of reaction to this situation which might be expected to appear. These we think might be the possible reactions of people who had committed no crimes.

Add now another factor. Take a roomful of human beings, of whom many have a streak of weakness in their nature. People who have had, in some cases, the misfortunes and handicaps of a bad home background. Imagine selfish people and greedy, or those whose motto in life has been 'What do I get out of this?' and include them in the new group. Some of these people would be those whose lives had been deprived of much that creates happiness for ordinary folk, and there might also be those who, through some physical handicap, had become embittered. There would be men and women who in childhood were entirely undisciplined, so that to hit out when frustrated was the natural pattern of their behaviour. Some would be the failures of life, people who never meant anything to anyone, and the aggressive, naughty child whom nobody loved enough to control and who had become a trouble-maker. Lazy people would be there, who were never made to do what they should, and pathetic people who never quite made the grade, and always got pushed around by others. Lastly there would be people who had done nothing wrong but had been unable to prove their innocence, though these would be but very few.

Such people, shut away for months and years, would be difficult to handle. Imagine, as we have, the reactions of the ordinary people, and then see this new group with all their handicaps and deprivations. It is easy to see the magnitude of the task which confronts the administrators of prisons, who must at the present time organize the lives of some 23,000 people, often in buildings entirely unsuited to the task, sometimes with the knowledge that the public are ready to pounce on them for any failure on their part to provide the complete safety and security demanded of them!

One factor must not be overlooked. Whereas the first

people would have had no previous experience of custody, and so would begin at the beginning, the second group would have amongst them some who had been in prison before and would know all the tricks. They would know how to get the best out of it, and whilst some might be easier to handle, there would be others who belonged to a hard core of recidivists, adept at evading the law and skilful in making difficulties in the smooth running of the institution.

Prisoners are ordinary people, but the majority of them have added handicaps which in many cases have accounted for the fact that they have taken to a life of crime. These difficulties of personality are not noticeable most of the time but only in certain circumstances and it is to overcome these personality twists and disorders that efforts must be made during the time that such people are in custody and afterwards on release.

Personal relationships between prisoners matter a great deal. In most of us there exists a wish to be appreciated and even admired by someone. Lucky free people find this in the close circle of their families, to whom they can go, confident that they will be understood and supported.

Not so in prison. Quite a number of prisoners have only their comrades to whom to turn for any need they may feel for companionship and sympathy. There is in most of us also a wish to be accepted by our companions, and often little exaggerations about home and family in order to 'keep up with the Jones's' are passed round. In prison this characteristic is even more marked and often quite fantastic stories are told over and over again to create a background which is very far from the real one.

A girl whom I remember many years ago came from one of the worst districts of one of our larger cities. Her parents had rejected her and she was alone without a friend or relative. Rather than admit so unhappy a fact

and accept the position of a nobody, she invented a house
with bay windows, one on each side of the front door,
which, she said, was her parents' home. So faithfully did
she describe this house that I can see it to this day, yet
there was no word of truth in the story. It was a lie, but
how much the thought of that dream house had meant
to that girl during years of loneliness. Many prisoners are
'showmen', some even come to believe in their own
stories after many repetitions, and some are vastly entertaining.

Another girl told of life as a child which had been
dominated by a father who was ex-army and a real
martinet—according to her story. It turned out that she
had really been left on a doorstep as a baby and never
knew her father. This same girl wept bitterly when, in
the days before the shortened birth certificate, she received
a full one with a space where the father's name should
have been. There are many who romance, and tell tales
of their own prowess and the big *jobs* they have pulled
off. It all helps to pass the time and some of the stories
help the little man to feel a bit better about his own
inadequacy.

'*Grassing*', or telling tales, is the worst sin that a prisoner
can commit, and a man or woman guilty of this may
indeed go in fear of a beating up by other prisoners. It
must be remembered that there are certain rigid standards
of behaviour in the closed community of a prison and
these standards must be kept, although they are not our
standards outside. To tell tales is disloyal, and loyalty of
a sort is very important to people in custody.

This loyalty expresses itself sometimes if the prison
officer, or '*screw*', in charge of the particular working party
is one who has earned respect. Men will play fair with
such an officer, as they will by a Governor who is understanding and just, however severe he may be.

No human being is all bad. In this respect many modern plays and books are unreliable and are obviously written by people who do not know the true facts. Most prisoners have their good qualities as well as the bad ones, and it is the duty and responsibility of those who talk about after-care to remember this, because it is on these good qualities that the future rehabilitation of that man or woman will depend.

Common to most men and women in custody is a general immaturity. This is very noticeable when they are first released. Once the freedom of choice is removed from an individual it seems that something ceases to grow up, so that men will come out after long sentences acting the age at which they first went in. This is one of the failures of the whole prison system and, until we can think of ways in which a man's dignity can be maintained during his time in custody, he will be unready to develop so that he can face the stresses and strains of outside life on release. This immaturity often expresses itself in a commonly seen characteristic whereby a man of mature years will revert to the dress and habits of the young man that he was when first sentenced and it would seem there is a need to live through all the stages that have been missed. The attitude of the released prisoner to 'them' and 'us' is always there in the background, particularly with the old lags. 'Them' is a term used to cover all those people on the right side of the law and a vast barrier exists between such people and themselves. Prisoners will always try to help each other after release, and I have frequently listened to comments about reports of crime in the newspapers when the ex-prisoner will say 'Hard Luck', or 'Poor old Taff', meaning the man on the run and not the victim.

This attitude is something that people outside find hard to accept. Yet it is natural that the ex-prisoner's outlook is bound to be influenced by his own feeling towards capture and his sympathy for his mates. It is only after years that the other side of the picture comes home.

Men who have served long sentences have often become institutionalized and they find it extremely difficult to adjust to outside life. For years old lags have not had to think for themselves, even the money that they earn in prison is paid out in kind for the small luxuries of life such as tobacco and little additions to the prison diet and is never used for actual payment of board and lodging, since the amounts are so small. It is therefore difficult, after many years, for a man to feel, on receiving his pay packet, that much has to come out for the cost of actual living before anything can be bought for himself in the way of tobacco or drink. So often good people who mean well get very distressed about the way in which money is wasted by ex-prisoners because they are thinking in terms of their own long practised economies and they fail to understand that the old lag has none of the same background nor experience of making ends meet. Learning to live on one's income is difficult enough for ordinary people, and it takes a long time before an ex-prisoner can adjust to this new responsibility after release. Great patience and understanding is necessary on both sides.

The fact that this responsibility for living is removed from people during custody means that there is far too much time to think about other things, and in prison the natural planning and organizing ability must then be turned towards outwitting authority, whilst in a world where there is no actual money to handle, '*snout*' becomes currency and men with ingenuity find ways and means of getting more than their fair share of this by forcing payment in tobacco for services rendered to another prisoner. It can happen that men have become involved with others in this way while serving their sentences and

C

it has made it harder for them to break free once they were released.

Sometimes people have made a great mistake in underrating the level of intelligence of men and women in prison. Many of them have been experts in the field of crime which they have pursued, and it is quite wrong to suppose that because a man is skilled at manipulating locks he is sub-normal in other matters. Although a man may be immature through the many years he has spent in custody, he may still be, and often is, capable beyond the average in providing himself with the wherewithal for his chosen way of life. Prisoners very greatly resent anyone who treats them as inferior and any patronising attitude on the part of people seeking to do after-care is disastrous.

Some indication has been given in this brief account of the difficulty in describing prisoners. There are people of all kinds and abilities inside, just as there are outside. To meet prisoners is to see men and women who appear just the same as ordinary people. Most of them have handicaps that are not apparent until one has known them for some time, and it is these limitations, due partly to their background and partly to the institutional life they have been forced to live, that create such vast problems.

To sum up this chapter I would like to give a few examples of the kind of people one might expect to meet in an ordinary prison where men or women are serving both long and shorter sentences, and where there are old lags as well as star prisoners. The people described are all real, although some of the facts which might give away their identity have been omitted.

Jo is a good looking man, well built and with a pleasant open face. He looks you straight in the eye when he speaks to you and his handshake is firm. The first impression of

Jo is of a straightforward man who must have been the victim of some dastardly plot, otherwise he would never have seen the inside of a prison. Get acquainted with Jo and watch his eyes. He will tell you about his life outside —the wife who left him—'Not her fault', he will say. 'Couldn't expect her to stick to a chap when he had let her down so badly.' Sometimes there is the photograph of the child shown to you when you go to see Jo, and you find your compassion aroused. Watch his eyes. The mouth may smile, the right thing be said, but few people can control the expression in their eyes. His attitude is one of deference and a touch of flattering humility to you—yes, it is all there. Now pull yourself together and think. Here is a man who would have no difficulty in getting a position of trust; he exudes confidence. You can picture him in an executive position running a business. You find yourself being persuaded, as have many others, to believe in him. Why? Jo is clever; he knows that you may be able to help him and so he is trying you out. Ignore the charm and make it clear that you are not impressed, and see what happens. Jo will leave you alone—you are no use to him, perhaps someone else will be more amenable.

Jo is a con man.

Now let us meet Harry. He looks rather pathetic at first sight. A plain, pale face, an honest and too readily expressed determination never to be a silly fool again. 'One thing I can promise you,' he says in the first five minutes, 'I've learned my lesson. I'm never going to see the inside of one of these places again.' Weak, vain, always ready to promise anything, Harry will be a difficult man to help. It takes character and great perseverance to go straight, and Harry lacks both these qualities. Watch him as soon as he is released. He must

have clothes—lots of them—possessions—all the things he
wants he must have, and so he has to pick up some money
to get them. He means to do just a few *jobs* to get this
money and then he thinks he'll have a try at going straight.
He does the *jobs* and if he is not caught he thinks it's easy
and it goes to his head. Soon he begins to think he's a
fine fellow, much cleverer than the police—a very dangerous supposition as many well know. Presently he needs
more money and he thinks 'Why not go on and get a bit
more whilst my luck holds? I can always give it up later
when I've pulled off a big one.' Harry is conceited and a
small man, and sooner or later he is certain to be careless
and be caught red-handed, so that back he goes to prison.
Once inside, the same old tale begins again—'I was a
fool—I promise you I'll never do it again—I'll never
come back here—I've had enough.'

Harry is a *recidivist*.

Sam is a difficult man to meet. He doesn't want visitors!
Why should he have some silly fool coming and telling
him what to do? 'They're all the same, these visitors,' he
says. 'They come to tell you that they're here to help
you—give you a lot of ruddy clap trap, Bible thumping
talk, and then the first time you don't suit them it's "Get
out"! No thank you, I'll fight my own battles, nobody's
going to do anything for me.' Sam thinks he can look
after himself. If you do get to see him he will say something
to shock you or test you, just to see how you'll react, and
your impression of Sam will be that he is interviewing
you and sizing you up. If you meet him as you walk
round the prison he will walk away if you show any
particular interest in what he is doing—he wants no truck
with a ruddy outsider—'They're all the same—no ruddy
good.' Sam is a difficult man, but probably you don't see,
unless you have the gift of imagination, that Sam has a

horribly vulnerable side. He has that one thing no prisoner wants to admit—he has a kind heart, and he really loathes himself for being in the position in which you see him, and has therefore tried to grow a hard shell in which he hides his true nature. He is suffering more than Jo or Harry because he has to live with himself inside that shell, and the memory of his own failures is with him all the time. You, by just coming to see him, make this contrast between the real Sam and the Sam who is in prison more marked, so he hates you and all you stand for. He has the guts to make good, if he had but the will and determination, and if one day he really decides to live differently he has the ability to do it, but in the meantime he is a most difficult and unco-operative prisoner.

Sam is a problem.

Eric is easy to talk to. He has a way with women, and is not a bad looking chap. There is something likeable about him from the first. No, he wouldn't be such a fool as to throw his chance away. He has a home somewhere and he's not going to let them down. As he continues to talk it becomes obvious that he thinks himself rather a fine chap; he must have a car—a good one—when he gets out, and of course he will have a holiday before he starts work. After all, he's earned it, hasn't he? Eric's ideas are all mixed up. He wants to run before he can walk. You begin to wonder where all the money will come from for all that he is going to do, and you are probably right in your supposition. 'I want, and I must have,' is his motto, and unless something happens to change his views here is a man lined up for another sentence before long. He is quite willing to have a visitor, for you will be just the audience for him and he will enjoy telling you all his big ideas. There are always some Erics in prisons, their stories are often quite untrue, and everyone knows it, but they are interesting and help to pass the time away. Eric comes to believe his stories in time, and he thinks he is a finer man than he really is, which is fatal for him when he comes out unless something can be done to make him realise his faults.

Eric is a showman.

Maureen is a different type. Like many of her kind her life's 'work' has started at a very early age. She is attractive in spite of the prison clothes, and it is easy to see the Maureen of the streets when you talk to her. Life in the city where Maureen lives is full of adventure to her, she is young still, young enough not to worry about the future. She has never had an ordinary honest job and anyway—how dull! This time in prison is a bore, but part of the price to be paid for the times in between. 'But why should I work in a factory?', she said to me one day in my office. 'I'd never get enough money even if I worked all the overtime there was. Don't you see that if I want to buy a new dress I can get enough in one night to buy it honest?' She has standards, even if not the right ones. You will like Maureen—she is warm-hearted and loyal to her friends, but she has been brought up to a way of life which is so remote from your own that you find much that she says to be completely revolutionary. You would like to help her, but the difficulty is that there is so little that you can think of that will provide enough excitement and colour in her life to make her see that it is worth while. Many worthy people think that all that is necessary for the Maureens of this life is to find a nice steady job—perhaps at cleaning—and then they'll be quite all right. If not, then they are ungrateful for all the help that has been given them. This sort of thinking does not touch the problem.

Maureen is a prostitute.

Old Sarah is quiet and well behaved inside. Her cell is beautifully clean and quite attractive. I found myself thinking she was just the type of woman I would like to employ as a 'daily'. We chatted about all sorts of things once she realized that I was friendly. Sarah was an abortionist. Very serious trouble had come from her previous exploits, people had been horrified and a jury had wasted no time in bringing in the verdict of 'Guilty'. Hers was a particularly depraved type of crime and the sooner she was shut away the better. To Sarah, however, it didn't seem like that. 'It's like this, deary,' she said. 'The likes of us is necessary as you might say. Oo's going to look after them young girls if it wasn't for us? Right it is, too, that they should pay well for it—after all, look at the risks we take.'

    Here is someone who sees crime differently.

Vera was beautiful. Even the ill-fitting cotton dress of the prison couldn't hide her elegant figure. Educated, reserved, efficient, her face registered no emotion at all. Courteous when spoken to, Vera was quite withdrawn, her almost insolent superiority put one at a disadvantage. 'What is this girl doing behind bars?' you wonder, but her record reveals a long list of skilfully planned hotel thefts. Vera was waiting—she could bide her time, she was waiting for release when money and pleasure would again be her lot. Meanwhile her talents were being used in the prison library, for Vera gave no trouble. She could do her work well and had no intention of losing any of her remission by bad behaviour, the sooner she could get out again the better.

    Vera is an extremely difficult con woman.

Bill and Walter were inseparable in my memory. I knew them both many years ago in one of our long-term prisons. They had a friendship which is sometimes found amongst people in custody and if you met them you would notice certain characteristics. Bill will talk to you about Walter—how he is getting on in the prison, how he is learning to do handicrafts, and Bill is always encouraging him. Bill will tell you that perhaps one day Walter's work will be recognized nationally, he has real talent and he will get on. 'The *screws* don't understand Walter,' Bill will say. 'They're always picking on him, but that's just because they're too stupid to understand what talent he has got. I understand him, and I am encouraging him to paint. One day everybody will know about Walter.' Bill has said nothing about himself, he is rather like a proud mother telling you about her only child, but when you meet Walter you will see a totally different kind of person from the picture that Bill has shown you. Walter is weak, shifty, and obviously very difficult. He depends on Bill, for without him he'd be nobody to anyone. He has no family, and no visitors; long ago rejected by his parents, he has drifted about, serving one sentence after another. Both these men have spent most of their lives in custody, from approved school they drifted to Borstal and then prison, and there seems little ahead except further trouble. They have been failures and it seems unlikely that either of them will be able to stay outside long. The world frowns on such friendships and with high-minded scorn turned down the second part of the Wolfenden report. What will happen to these two in the end? Both Bill and Walter are unloved by anyone else, but they have found some semblance of happiness in their illicit relationship and are harming nobody. Understanding authority had not been too censorious, but of course—it can't be allowed to go on—when it becomes too obvious punishment must be meted out. Since Bill and Walter must be separated and cannot be allowed to live together as they like when they are released, it may be that children will be the sufferers from their compulsions towards an unnatural life, but that is in the future.

Bill and Walter are homosexuals.

The tale could go on. Type after type could be described, the Sams, the Jos, the Maureens, could be multiplied a hundred times, and all the varying people who are a mixture of these and other characters. Some are hardly criminal at all, others so twisted as to be almost impossible. Varying as they do from one another, yet how like in many ways to people outside whose true characteristics never come to light because they are never caught.

Shut away from society it is inevitable that such people should exert an influence on each other. Day after day they are thrown together without outside influences, and all these men and women will one day be free. It is unlikely that the effect of association with other difficult people will do much towards rehabilitation and so we must look to the other influences that will shape the lives of these people during their time in custody.

3

AFTER-CARE BEGINS

It may appear from what follows that I am writing solely from the point of view of the prisoner, and that I have forgotten the public who have been robbed, beaten up, or suffered other terrible things at the hands of dangerous men. This is not so. I am well aware that it is necessary to protect the public and to see that the perpetrators of crime are put where they can do no further harm.

The purpose of this book is to draw attention to the fact that once sentence has been passed, and a decision has been taken as to the best punishment to mete out to the wrong-doer, unless he is to be hanged for murder there will come a day at the end of his sentence when he will walk out of the prison doors a free man.

This is happening every day. The man at your table in the café may have been a safe-breaker, or have been detained in connection with offences against children, or have hit an old lady over the head and taken her handbag. This is fact, not fiction. In time everyone comes out of prison, and in time each must make a fresh start either with or without help. If the start is to be a good one it will depend not on the influence of the other prisoners so much as the character and outlook of the ordinary men and women, both inside the prison and the public outside, who have exerted an influence for good or bad.

If something is to be done so that prisoners when they return to society are no longer to be the danger to others that they were in the past, then it is no good harbouring thoughts of revenge and hatred, as this only breeds violence and crime. What we must do is to think constructively so that from the moment a man or woman enters prison the work of rehabilitation must begin, and the building up process must be put in train; otherwise we are only making even more dangerous and anti-social people than we originally put in prison.

People who have committed crimes and leave the Court under sentence of imprisonment have, for the time being, lost everything. They walk down the steps from the dock to wait in the cells below for the police van to take them to the local gaol. They may, if families are waiting in Court, have an opportunity of seeing the wife or the girl friend through the bars before they depart. Difficult and often tearful farewells are said and they are often numb from the whole proceedings that have taken place in Court. They are herded together with other people under sentence, some pleased to have got off with so little, some knocked over by the length of the sentence imposed, whilst others rave at the injustice they think they have suffered, a few being just apathetic. The new man doesn't know what is coming, and he is probably frightened, though he cannot admit it. He has nothing to do, nothing more to decide, he is just a nobody who will be told what to do, pushed around and have to try and make the best of it. Probably he has well deserved the sentence he has received, and anyway the people upstairs have already forgotten him—there is another case being tried. Soon the Judge will go home to his dinner and the people will go away to their homes, and the prisoner is on his own with nothing to think about.

Following his arrival at the prison there are many delays. He has to go through reception where his clothes will be taken away from him, his personal possessions listed and put away after he has signed for them, in case he pretends there was some article there which he never owned. He must wait and wait and wait. Part of the time he is sitting in a little reception cell alone, trying to take in the printed list of prison rules and regulations hanging on the back of the door. He must wait for a bath, which will be run for him—the taps being on the outside —and any officer can look in and see him naked. He must be weighed and examined by the prison doctor, and he is given prison clothes and a number. All his one-time self respect is gone, if he had much. He may be miserable, truculent, aggressive, rude or indifferent, but he has nothing he can give anyone, nothing he can do except what he is ordered. He is no longer free.

The great Alexander Paterson once said you can't train a man for freedom in captivity, and how true this is.

The people whom the prisoner will now meet inside the prison must do what can be done to try and build him up again and make him feel that although he has nothing now, at least it is not too late to become a real person again one day.

Much of this work is the duty and responsibility of those who run our prisons, and they are well aware of the size of the task they have to undertake, but after the sentence is finished then we must do our share to help ex-prisoners to get back amongst us.

To help anyone it is first necessary to understand them. Indeed it is even more than that. To help anyone it is necessary to like them and to see in them the men and women they might have been and might still be. To begin to understand we must look at the outside people who influence the lives and characters of prisoners during the time they are in custody. These men and women have the first chance to do something to lay the foundations of a better life.

If a man or woman is kept in prison for a long period,

and during that time is regarded as less than human—a number, and not a person—then it must be obvious that he or she cannot, on walking out of the prison door, suddenly resume a rightful position as a good citizen.

One of the hopeful factors in today's prison system is the appointment of welfare officers in prisons. A welfare officer is a trained social worker and up to now appointments have been made by Discharged Prisoners' Aid Society. He is not part of the ordinary staff, but works full time within the prison. His duty is concerned with the welfare of the prisoner, his adjustment to his family, and often his future employment. The welfare officer is available to be seen on request, and it is good to know that because of the fine calibre of many welfare officers and their devotion to duty an increasing number of men and women consult them about their personal problems. Welfare officers work with the prison staff in arranging and planning pre-release courses, and are in touch with the families and with outside employers and Probation Officers. Their presence in prisons has already made a marked difference to the men and women in custody, and, although it is often discouraging work, they are tackling it with energy and enthusiasm.

It is easy to see that in a large prison with several hundred people one Welfare Officer has more than enough to do, and if all the prisoners wanted to see him his life would be quite impossible. Approach to the welfare officer is voluntary, and as so often happens certain prisoners who greatly need help are unwilling to ask for it. In spite of this a vast amount of good has been done since welfare officers became part of the team.

Prison chaplains are always a very important part of the rehabilitative staff of every prison. There is an Anglican padre and also a visiting Roman Catholic priest. Other denominations have their visiting ministers and every man or woman can be seen by a minister of his or her own faith. The local Rabbi also visits any Jews who may be in prison, but their numbers are commendably small, since the family ties are often much closer in good Jewish homes and parents discipline their children.

The task of the prison chaplain is an exceedingly difficult one. The prison is no ordinary parish and the prisoners live in a small world where they feel their needs are of the greatest importance and cannot understand how busy a part-time chaplain may be with the other duties he has to undertake. Many are suspicious of religion and the chaplain often starts at a great disadvantage because of this. In the old days a man often got the job of prison chaplain just because he lived near the prison and perhaps had time to pull in the extra work, or just needed the small stipend such duties warranted. Nowadays there is a far greater realization and understanding of the enormous difficulty and responsibility of the task, and more care is taken in the selection of men to serve in this way.

Preaching to prisoners, and visiting them in their cells, is an extremely difficult task, requiring great tact and understanding. A large number of prisoners are always ready to give lip-service to the demands of religion. It helps to pass the time, and 'anyway, the chaplain may be able to make things a bit easier for you if you turn up regularly and look interested', some have said.

Church attendance being voluntary, it is extremely difficult to know how to get the men who really need the church, and what it stands for, to attend. As things are it often means that those who really ought to be there are not. If it is compulsory then the men are hostile.

In writing of religion in prison it must be said that it is always the character of the chaplain that really matters. He must first be a man who can be respected for himself and not only for his cloth. He must be fair and above reproach, and his private life must match his public work so that no one can say 'Look at old so and so!! He can preach but look how he lives!'

Prisoners have ways and means of finding out about people and woe betide anyone whose private life is unworthy of his high calling. The padre who has the attitude 'You're not worth bothering about' is easily detected by the prisoner. I remember one man who was told 'I'm a busy man. I've got something else to do besides seeing you', and although this was very true, a prisoner, because of his limited world, cannot see it and feels that the chaplain is not really interested.

To many prisoners the padre is an enemy. He represents to those who have no religion a body of people who live comfortably and tell others what to do and how to behave. The chaplain will be well tested, he may be sure of that. No dogmatism or pious pronouncements will find a place with his prison congregation, and what he does will matter far more than what he says.

Prisoners all know that the chaplain draws a fee for his work and, therefore, having no understanding of the great difficulty many padres have in living on their small stipends, they become suspicious. How often I wish that the pay for all ministers of religion could be such that it was adequate for their great work and then they would not need the extra small amounts payable for duties in prisons and hospitals. It would then give them greater opportunities because they would be met with less suspicion.

The religious approach to a prisoner is a very difficult one. A man once said to me 'Religion makes you feel bad if it gets anywhere', and I know what he meant. A man in prison has to build a hard shell round his emotions. He has to adjust himself to the conditions under which he must live while he is inside, and he dare not let his feelings lie too near the surface. Religion reaches out through the emotions to the very heart of a man if it is to be effective, yet, as good chaplains know, a man must be treated very gently if this hard barrier is to be broken down and something good and constructive put in its place. Unless the religious approach can stimulate his courage and determination for good, it only leaves him emotional and at the mercy of other people. He must never be left feeling low and vulnerable if he is to survive his years of imprisonment, because in that way he cannot do his sentence. Condemnation only brings opposition, and soul-searching without comfort exposes him to more than he can bear. It is difficult to imagine how hard the padre's task is, and what special gifts he requires for such exacting work. People outside have so many other factors which interest and absorb them but the prisoner has hours in which to think, and often no one in whom to confide.

Another outside contact for many prisoners is the prison visitor. Many people of good will voluntarily carry out this work and do it well. One can meet many ex-prisoners who owe a great deal to the friendly visitor who has come regularly and listened to them, rather than talked—who has been really interested, and on release has continued this friendship.

It is not easy to be the right kind of visitor. Most people who do this work are actuated by the highest ideals, and yet there are some worthy Christian people who fail to make the right approach. There are people who are so anxious to get over the idea of Christian love and forgiveness that they forget that they are talking to people to whom the whole idea of Christianity is totally different from their own.

If a man or woman has had a pagan up-bringing, the idea of Christianity is that it is a sort of escapism into a fairy tale life by which people deceive themselves about true facts. Unfortunately there are always people who, whilst attending Church regularly and giving lip-service to the ethics of Christianity, are far from Christian in their private lives. Men and women in prison immediately scent hypocrisy and are antagonistic.

A man's ideas about the Fatherhood of God are bound to be influenced by the kind of picture conjured up by the word 'father'.

There is the prisoner's own idea about his life of crime. Why should he want to be forgiven if he has convinced himself that he was perfectly right in what he did?

This is by no means to convey the impression that the Christian approach is the wrong one. It all depends what the visitor thinks the Christian approach really is. All too often our ideas on this subject are our own and not really drawn from the Great Example. A glance at the Gospels will quickly show that Jesus talked with many people about simple things and about the work they were doing, so that people were attracted first by His personality.

Prisoners have received much help by having visits from someone whose warm sympathy made him the ideal listener. Of course the visitor is going to hear a number of extremely doubtful tales. He himself is going to be tested and the prisoner—if he cares at all—wants to see how much he is going to be believed. The good listener, not the critic or the obvious 'do-gooder', is the ideal guest.

One prisoner told me a story of great appreciation about a dear elderly gentleman who visited him for years. This man must have been the ideal prison visitor. The prisoner in question was a difficult man, rather like Sam described in an earlier chapter. He enjoyed a good discussion but sometimes he got angry with his visitor and even on occasions ordered him to go. Yet this gentleman never gave up, and time and time again he would call, even making long journeys to see his friend. Years later

D

that prisoner told me of what he owed to his visitor. He said 'Mr X will never know what it meant to me—he never gave me up even when I was rude to him. He always came back.'

A prisoner has a visitor only if he agrees to have one. This means that it is another of the few things in which he can exercise his will power in a life which is almost always completely organized. He MUST see the chaplain at some time, but he needn't have a visitor. Consequently many refuse—not because a visitor is not really wanted, but because it is a way of asserting independence.

Sometimes someone suggests that it might be useful to have a friend outside and a man will elect to accept a visit, or he may be just curious, or feels it will help to pass the time. Whatever the reason for a man's agreeing to have a visitor it is frequently not the true motive behind the decision. No one wants to admit that he is lonely and longs to see someone. Some avoid all such contacts because the contrast between the life of the visitor and their circumstances makes the present even more unbearable.

In a long-term prison the question of visitors is often very tricky. In these prisons the men are living for years in a very small world, so that everything that happens in it is of extreme importance to them. It may well happen that someone in the workshop or on the landing has mocked at the idea of having visitors, so the weak man dare not agree to have one. The most powerful directive in his life is the fear of losing the approbation of the men with whom he spends most of his time.

I remember one man whom I visited for many years in such a prison. Every now and then he would write and say I needn't come any more. I knew he didn't mean it, but for some reason unknown to me he found it embarrassing at the time. I always continued to write to him, and later on I would receive a letter saying 'You can come and see me again now if you like.' In this case I found out long afterwards from the Governor that the particular prisoner who had caused the trouble about receiving visitors had now gone out, so my man could resume his contact with me.

If a visitor has to visit a prison where there is a man he knows, he must respect the prisoner's right to refuse to see him.

Another responsibility the visitor has is of seeing that his prisoner never loses face. Some good people will PROBE. They want to know all sorts of private and personal things about the man they are visiting—things they would never dream of asking their acquaintances outside. Men have told how visitors often want to know about the crimes they have committed in all detail, or they ask impertinent questions about sex. In fact some visitors have shown by their questions and their whole attitude that they think they are talking to some poor creature who is inferior. People have felt that if the prisoner can be reduced to a state of emotionalism in order to get some confession, that it is the right thing. What a terrible mistake. Emotionalism rarely helps. Probing may satisfy the visitor, but the recipient always suffers.

Questions about crimes and sentences are not wanted; if they are asked it is more than likely that they will be answered with a lie. Other visitors have been known to spend all the time talking about themselves, and using the prisoner, who cannot get away, as an audience.

When they are nearing the end of a long sentence some men are given the hostel scheme, where they work outside, as ordinary wage earners, but live within the prison hostel. Sometimes they live too far from their homes to make week-end visits to their families. Other men are homeless. If for any reason a man cannot avail himself of the opportunity of going home, he is asked if he would like instead to have a visitor.

I knew one outsider who undertook the care of such a man. He was obviously good hearted, but entirely without imagination. He offered to call for his prisoner and take him for a walk on a Sunday afternoon to see the streets and buildings of the city where he lived; a rather dreary occupation at the best of times. A hostel man is free to go out in the evenings and he knows the city streets quite well. Had he been invited to tea at the visitor's home it would have been far better, because that would have made him feel accepted. It is the difference between being at the receiving end of charity and being treated as a guest. One has to be so careful to avoid even the semblance of charity in visiting prisoners who have nothing to give in return.

The prison visitor is a really important person, but like the chaplain the thing that matters is the man himself. If he exercises tact and understanding he is acceptable and can bring much pleasure and friendship to the prisoner, but he must be genuine, otherwise he is more harmful than helpful.

Another group of outside people who come in contact with the prisoners are the educational staff. These men and women visit the prison to conduct classes in the evenings on a great variety of subjects, or they may be part of the prison staff giving instruction in brick-laying, painting and decorating, building and many other trades to help a man get a job on release.

Wherever possible work is found for everybody, and with the maintenance of the prison buildings, the laundry, the kitchen, as well as the workshops there is quite a lot to do. Unfortunately it is still not possible to employ all men for eight hours a day because of shortage of staff and overcrowding.

It has been mentioned in the chapter on prisons that certain people who get sent to prison are illiterate. This is not always because they are of low intelligence, but often because of the lack of discipline or parental interest which has accounted for truancy from school. Much time that should have been spent on acquiring knowledge has been wasted. Probably most people outside owe their education to the fact that they had the kind of parents who saw to it that their children attended school regularly and were interested in what they were doing.

If a grown man or woman is illiterate it is a serious handicap. To cover up this difficulty some have taken to crime and because they have felt handicapped they have found other means of expressing their personalities. If such a man or woman can be taught to read and write, new possibilities are open and a feeling of equality with others will sometimes turn a delinquent into a good citizen.

Tutorial staff in a prison need to be tactful. Amongst their classes will be many people of varying intelligence. Some have only reached the educational standards of children but they are not children and they are not mentally defective. Nothing is more harmful to the re-habilitation of a prisoner than to be treated as a child or a half-wit. The task of the tutor is to try and repair the gaps in the education whilst remembering that a man who is skilled in his chosen profession—even if that profession is burglary—is no fool, and will take a dim view of his tutor if he is treated like one. It is difficult, whilst giving fairly simple instruction to some member of the group, to hold the interest of the highly intelligent and well read prisoner who may also be in the class.

Medical staff in a large prison are often full time, but in the majority of smaller prisons one of the local doctors and dentists will pay regular visits.

Contact with the medical staff is another outside

contact, and is therefore again an influence on the prisoner's life and can be of great importance in his after-care. Ideas of the genuine interest a doctor has in his patient are formed during a long sentence, and a man who knows that he has had the best attention that a patient can get, even though he is a prisoner, builds up a respect and appreciation for the medical services and doctors in general.

There have been doctors in the past who have not always regarded the prisoner as an ordinary human being, and have not realized that he is just as sensitive to pain and illness as an outside patient. In the few instances where this has happened the effect on the prisoner has been far more damaging than if he had been free. If he is 'only a prisoner' and feels that the doctor or dentist is always in a hurry to get rid of him, he naturally resents it and such treatment can turn an inmate into a difficult and obstructive man.

Outside people can change their doctors and dentists. The prisoner is completely at the mercy of his medical staff. He has certain rights, in that he can complain to the Governor or the visiting magistrate, but even if his story sounds authentic and it is different from the opinion of a highly respected member of the medical profession, how much credence can be extended to the prisoner who has probably been known as a liar on other occasions?

This all goes to show how immense is the responsibility resting on the outside people who have the first opportunity of influencing prisoners during their time in custody and before the real after-care begins.

Of course, it is inevitable that some prisoners will do their best to play tricks on the medical staff, as on other people, and one has to be wise to this.

I am reminded of a man who played a really amazing trick on the doctor in one of our larger prisons a few years ago. This prisoner was an extremely ingenious man and clever with his hands, and as his time was not fully occupied he thought out many ideas to pass the time, one of which was to keep an eye on certain prison officers in their leisure hours. As this meant watching over a considerable distance he very much wanted a small telescope. He thought out a plan to make one, but he needed a very strong lens, and naturally such things are not supplied to prisoners. Although his eyesight was excellent, he applied to the doctor for reading glasses, complaining that he couldn't see to read properly in his cell. In due course he had his opportunity and an arrangement was made for his eyes to be tested.

His memory was retentive and he soon learned the letters on the doctor's chart, and armed with this knowledge he pretended to be unable to see through the ordinary lenses given to him to test. At last, when the doctor produced the strongest lenses he'd got, the prisoner suddenly found himself able to see and 'read' the letters perfectly, although in fact by this time he could see nothing at all.

Armed with the strongest pair of reading glasses he could get, and a toilet roll he had acquired, he made the telescope which provided a great deal of information about the distant movements of the staff off duty!

Clever men, with nothing to fill their minds during long periods of confinement, are ingenious to a degree most people outside prison would hardly credit.

We have now looked briefly at some of the contacts a prisoner makes with outside people during his time in custody, but by far the most important is that of the prison officer. Every day, everywhere he goes, the officers will be there, and this means that on them rests the greatest responsibility of all for the early stages of after-care.

Careful selection goes on when a man or woman applies for the job of a prison officer, and it is important to screen the candidates as well as possible so that people of known bad character are excluded, and there is no place for those whose previous lives have been unsatisfactory. If accepted for training a candidate is first attached to his local prison where he begins his instruction in the duties and responsibilities of his office.

After serving some months during this probationary period he may even then not be recommended to go to the Officers' Training School, but if he does make the grade he will then have three months' intensive training for his future post.

There is much to be learned which might be called the mechanics of the job. He must be physically fit, proficient in the art of judo, know how to apply handcuffs, how to search a prisoner, and of course all the rules and regulations governing prisons and his approach to the prisoner.

In the old days the prison officer was only to be a custodial officer and nothing more. He was there to see that the prisoner did not escape and that he carried out the programme of work and exercise laid down for him. He was not permitted to speak to the men in his care, and as long as he did this job satisfactorily that was all that was required of him.

In recent years a totally different conception of the function of the prison officer has taken place, and it is now the generally accepted ideal that prison should be reformative if possible, and that the rehabilitation of the inmates is the thing that really matters. It is therefore a totally different concept for young trainees today from that of their predecessors. The officer has this new approach to make to his work, and still must know all that is necessary to carry out his custodial duties. In the nineteenth century an officer could be a brutish sort of man, with little intelligence, providing he could keep the prisoners in their place, but today he must be a man of considerable intelligence and tact if he is to fulfil his highly important role.

The transition period has not been easy. Good custodial officers of the old days must have found the change an extremely difficult one, for it takes a very fine personality to be able to adjust to new conditions. Some have done this remarkably well, and wonderful progress has been made in many institutions, but naturally there have been some who found the change not only difficult, but almost impossible.

I have been associated with a great many prisons in different ways for many years, and I have admired and respected many fine officers who are doing a real service for the people in their care, but because a prison is such a small world, even one man or woman who does not measure up to the high standards of the job can do a great deal of harm. Again the really important thing is what kind of a man or woman the prison officer is.

The position is one carrying great power. The officer will be constantly with people who are not in a position to contradict him or oppose his will. If they do then they will be punished. He will have men under him who must obey his command, and unlike an officer in the army, these men in his 'regiment' have very few rights; no member of the public will be present to see what he is doing, and, because of his position and status, in any disagreement between himself and a prisoner it is more likely that his word will be taken than that of the other man.

Power can be a great temptation. It is tremendously important that this power should be exercised properly, for the prison officer has more than usual opportunities for its mis-use. Hence the careful selection and the wide training.

The public do not always give the prison officer his rightful place in society. He does a difficult and exacting job and he should be regarded in a very different light from that which exists in the minds of many people. If a prison officer feels that he is not accepted socially because of the work he does, then there is an even greater temptation to mis-use power, and it is highly important that everything should be done to make such men and women feel they are respected by the public for the fine work they do.

One ex-prisoner told me of an incident during a long sentence when he was feeling mentally disturbed due to frustration and worry over an injustice he felt he had suffered. It was evening, and he was almost at breaking point; his mood was an ugly one, and he determined to take some action to relieve his pent-up feelings. Coming down the stairs from one of the landings he walked right into an officer. Had this man been a bad officer there might have been an incident with violence. Instead it was an officer who had been fair and was respected by the men. 'If you hadn't been a good 'un I'd kicked you right in the air,' said the prisoner, almost beside himself at the time, but the danger passed and all was well. Outside we cannot realise, as the prison staff know so well, that there are moments of tension in many prisoners' lives when one wrong word, or one wrong action, will provide the final straw for a man suffering from strain.

This can be well illustrated by a story of a very different kind. It can be told now because the officer and the prisoner have long since gone, but it shows the need for the very careful policy of those in authority to select only the most suitable candidates for this special work.

A certain man had been in prison for many years, and

throughout the whole of his sentence had suffered from the embarrassment of haemorrhoids. Outside this would have been difficult enough, but in prison the problem of changing clothing when necessary and getting short times off from work was extremely difficult. On one occasion the sympathy and understanding of an excellent works officer saved what might have been a terrible situation. The prisoner was in the clothing store getting a necessary change of garments when an officer of the type who should never have been in a prison at all brought a group of men into the building. Seeing the embarrassing situation, and also seeing an opportunity of amusing the men in his group, he picked up a soiled garment and displayed it to the men with a ribald joke. That officer's life was in real danger for a matter of minutes, and had it not been for the quick action of the responsible instructor murder might have been done.

Humour of any sort at the expense of a human being who cannot retaliate is not only wrong but cruel and dangerous. Sarcasm also is a weapon which should never be used on a prisoner. There are few occasions in ordinary life when sarcasm is effective or necessary, but never in a prison.

The wrong use of humour has often caused trouble. In the outside world a teacher may say teasingly to a group of young people that if a certain football team fails to win a match he'll see they all get into trouble. Everyone can laugh, because they know very well the man is joking and he neither can nor would do anything to them. Yet years ago, an officer in one of our prisons would regularly say to his men 'If Chelsea doesn't win today I shall *nick* you'. This in prison language meant that he would report them for misbehaviour and they would suffer punishment, and the men in that particular prison never knew whether he meant it. Such jibes are unworthy and belong to a past age when the prisoner's future did not matter to the officers.

It would be useless to write about after-care without some recognition of the immense task that the staff of a prison face in avoiding all that would undermine confidence and cause even more difficulty than the inmates are already facing.

Unwise remarks, even said in a teasing vein, can do great harm. I know one officer who would relieve the boredom of reception by joking comments on the faces of the men waiting to come into the prison. No doubt he thought he was being funny, and another of the reception officers might have thought so too, but when he said to one of the men 'I don't like your face and I'll see you get nicked' it was not funny at all. The prisoner was feeling far from humorous, he was at his lowest, having just come from the Court where he had received a long sentence, and was in no mood to realise that the officer had made a joke. Later, if that particular officer had occasion to report the man he would remember and he would almost certainly feel that the officer was carrying out his threat. Such news travels round a prison very quickly, and can give an officer a bad name. Stories that are passed round tend to grow as they travel and one can quickly see how easily an officer can get on the wrong side of the men through a foolish joke, and make dangerous enemies without realising it.

There is a wise rule in all prisons that an officer must not touch a prisoner. This is much more important than many people realise because a jolly slap on the back which a man outside can give another and no harm done can very easily be exaggerated to appear like a cuff, and the news would fly round the prison. Another kind of danger in this small world could be the officer who, with the best of intentions, might lay a comforting hand on the shoulder of a prisoner who was distressed. This could be made to appear like a demonstration of affection between the two men, and in the suspicions and intrigues of the prison could soon amount to a homosexual approach.

There are so many difficulties for the new recruit to learn to appreciate, and much he can only acquire through experience and through the wise help of older men in the service. A new man joining his first prison is likely to arrive full of enthusiasm for his work, and full of ideas as to the way in which he will carry it out. He is almost certain to meet a few older officers who will soon try to knock those new-fangled ideas out of him and some have succeeded in doing this. However, the new way has come to stay and the responsibility for new recruits is to remember what they have learned in their training and to see that they carry out their instructions to the best of their ability no matter what other influences may be brought to bear on them.

Things which seem mere incidents and of no particular importance outside a prison become magnified enormously inside. I remember hearing about a new Governor, a man's man, who took over one of the most difficult prisons for long term and hard core prisoners. Walking round the prison soon after he arrived he saw in one building a small party of men had been working on a painting job for some hours. It was the time for the officer to have his tea break and the Governor noticed that only this one man was having tea. Immediately the new Governor gave orders that the men on this special work were also to have a tea break, since they had been doing the actual painting whilst the officer was merely looking on, as was his duty. This tale flew round the prison and has been told on several occasions, by different men who were there at the time, for it did much to establish a good relationship with the new Governor for his fairness and consideration. The Governor himself paid for that tea on the first occasion, but it became an established custom that future parties doing special work would all share the tea break as a matter of course.

Prison Officers in the higher ranks may have the duty of censoring letters. There is a rule that all letters written and received by a prisoner must be censored in order to prevent plotting with outside people for escape, or for smuggling things into the institution. It is necessary that this should be done because of the small proportion of men and women who would use this means to further such ends, and so all prisoners have to suffer. It is something which never ceases to be a cause of irritation and distress to them as it would to any of us. It means that a prisoner writing to his family is aware that everything he says will be known to the censoring officer, and it is vitally important that the rule is observed which forbids such an officer to divulge to any other the contents of the letters he has to see. Only if there is something damaging to security or of considerable concern to the prisoner may he consult anyone about these matters, and then only the Governor. The fact that even one censoring officer has ever abused such a privilege and referred to a private matter has caused some prisoners to feel that all censors share information with other people. This is not true, and there are only rare incidents where a responsible person has abused his trust. There is another reason for the careful scrutiny of letters as well as the security risk. I know cases where it has been a real safeguard. For instance, a foolish and thoughtless writer from the outside may suggest that a prisoner's wife is not all that she ought to be. Quite possibly the information may have been wrong, but even if true the effect on a man in custody is disastrous and could cause him to attempt to escape or behave violently. Such a letter needs investigation and sometimes welfare officers can be brought in to help so that a prisoner can learn of worrying news in the kindest possible way. The utmost care is taken in most prisons to see that great kindness is used when bad news has to be broken to a person in custody. News of the death of a loved one, or the unfaithfulness of a spouse, or serious illness at home, causes far deeper suffering to someone who has little else to think about and cannot go and find out for himself.

Often when I go round a prison I marvel at the good temper and good sense which is shown by the staff about the men in their charge. If a teacher loses his temper with his pupils it is a bad thing, and may cause some temporary distress. It may even result in the parents coming to the school and taking the matter up with the headmaster. Usually things can be straightened out and often it is all due to a misunderstanding. After all, teachers are human and anyone can lose his temper, for few people suffer fools gladly. The foreman at work may be known as a difficult and choleric man, and those who work in his shop usually get some fun out of telling tales about him at home, or in the pub, after which the matter can often be forgotten. This is not so in a prison. Imagine the responsibility resting on an officer that he must never lose control, even for a moment, nor in any circumstances use bad language in his dealing with the prisoners. The majority of officers manage very well to carry out this restraint, no matter what the provocation, but there are those few who fail and it is always with disastrous results. Most prison visiting magistrates are familiar with the application from a man or woman who reports that a certain officer swore at or struck the prisoner. Occasionally the prisoner is known to be a 'moaner', a man who is always complaining, and it may seem to the magistrates that the right is on the side of the officer. However, there are cases where it is obvious that the prisoner is telling the truth and there have been cases where it has been necessary for the officer to be dealt with for a breach of behaviour. Sometimes an officer has been transferred to another prison if such is the case, but news flies round and the man will always be suspect. Bad incidents are not always reported. There have been men in the service who have betrayed their trust and have gone into a man's cell in the evening, together with one or two other officers, and roughly handled a prisoner, even injuring him. Such injuries have subsequently been reported to the medical staff as self-inflicted.

It is an extraordinarily difficult thing to know how best these isolated incidents can be dealt with because so many prisoners are known to exaggerate. I have had much to do with men and women who have served prison sentences, over the past fifteen years, and it is with the greatest reserve that I record any such stories, only where I am absolutely satisfied that I have heard the exact truth.

The fact that some sadism and some mental cruelty exists is always in the minds of those in authority, and I know how careful they are that any such incident should be discovered and dealt with but the harm that such rare occurrences do to the attitude of all the prisoners is immeasurable. Since this book is primarily to point out and enumerate some new ways in which after-care can be strengthened and assisted, it must be recorded that there are occasional incidents where prisoners meet people in authority and people from the outside world who themselves are unworthy and thus embitter the prisoners. Such rare incidents make a whole lot of people less responsive and receptive to the after-care that is provided for them.

I will record one story which I know to be true through the sad incidents that followed. It concerns a young woman prisoner of most pleasing appearance who was doing a sentence of three years. She had had the misfortune to become involved in a life of crime at a fairly early age, and finally when still in her twenties had been sentenced to imprisonment. She was an extremely shy and fearful girl in many ways, and had suffered more from her dock appearance than most other people, for the eyes of many in court had been focused on her, and she had found herself unable to speak or move. Years later I heard of this girl again but it was the sad news that she had suffered a complete mental breakdown and was in an institution, unlikely to recover. It was through one of her associates that I learned of the experiences that led to her final illness. During her time in prison she had been singled out for certain duties where she was 'on show' when visitors were about the prison. 'Phoebe', as I will call her, would be sent for to serve meals to official visitors and to carry trays and jugs from the kitchen. A woman in authority in the prison had lost no opportunity of using sarcasm to Phoebe and had continually picked on her in front of visitors, causing untold suffering. 'Well, Phoebe,' she would say if the girl dropped something in her nervousness, 'Is that how they taught you to do things in your school?'—and again, when Phoebe had blundered into a chair and spilled tea in a saucer, 'You must excuse Phoebe—she will learn in time. She is not serving her boy friends in the night club now.' I know there are people who believe this kind of raillery may have the effect of making a person more careful and more controlled, but whatever the reason, in time Phoebe broke down completely and became one of the tragedies of the system.

The incidents about which I have written are fortunately the exception and there are many fine men and women who deserve nothing but admiration in the service

E

of our prisons. As in the case of the chaplains, the tutors, the medical staff and visitors, it is the character and quality of the men and women themselves which influence those with whom they come in contact, for good or ill. Many a prisoner remembers with gratitude and affection those members of staff who have been an example by their fairness and sympathy, and it is often the case that a man will ask me to convey a message of this nature to an officer in a prison he may know I am visiting. 'If you see old Jones when you go to "X" will you tell him I'm doing all right,' is often said, and it is good to see with what pleasure such messages are received by the officer.

These men and women of the prison service begin the duty of after-care and when they fulfil their arduous work with honest humanity they are doing something for the future of the human beings in their care. They can walk about the prison unafraid, for whatever a prisoner's faults his sense of loyalty is such that a good *screw* can count on it whatever happens. I have often had a prisoner say to me of a much respected officer, 'We'd never play up with him, it might get him into trouble.'

One day a young Borstal girl, telling me some stories of planned escapes, spoke of one scheme that had been arranged to take place when a certain small party of girls was being conducted to a clinic for special treatment. The day arrived and instead of the officer who should have been there another arrived who was greatly loved by the girls. 'So you see, we couldn't do it,' said my informant. 'Why not?' I enquired. 'Well, you see Miss Y. is so nice and we wouldn't run off from her party—it might make it awkward for her.'

Affection for certain prison officers by no means implies that they are lenient. On the contrary, I have known some popular officers with a very great reputation for severity in their dealings with the prisoners, but if a man or woman can be honestly described as a 'devil', but a 'just devil', then this officer can still command respect.

Prison is not meant to be a 'piece of cake'. After all, men and women are sent there because the public have demanded a system whereby those who offend against society must be put away where, at least for the time, they can do no more harm. Reformation comes through contact with people worthy of respect, and sincerity, fairness and just dealing are of the utmost importance in re-directing lives and so inevitably creating better citizens for the future.

After-care should only be a continuation of a process which has already begun. The moment when a sentenced man walks down the steps to the cells below the Court is the moment when every human being with whom he comes in contact will influence his future for good or ill.

In spite of some criticism a tribute must be paid to those wise and good-living people who, in whatever capacity they come in contact with prisoners, by their lives and influence have helped many men and women to return to society with a different outlook on life after release.

4

PRE-RELEASE

It will be necessary now to look at the steps that are taken by the Prison Department to prepare men for the change from prison life to freedom.

In England some of the most advanced thinking has been done, and each year new factors come to light and new opportunities are made for improvement. Pre-release work is always under review, and now that we have an Institute of Criminology at Cambridge much study has resulted in new ideas, and improvements are always being introduced.

In the old days nothing of the sort was undertaken and men and women on release from prison were turned out on to the streets with no preparation at all. It was realised that the chance of such people ever making good was extremely remote and although little can yet be done for the very short sentence prisoners at least a great deal is being done for those serving longer sentences. There is still a great deal more to be achieved, but things are moving and the whole position is constantly under review.

First of all, something must be said about the classifying system that has been in operation for some years. Originally all people in custody went to the nearest prison, whether they were men, women or children. The first reforms were directed towards separating the sexes and then separating entirely the very young offenders from older people. One of our oldest prisons still has a wing which was at one time entirely used for the confinement of children, and the doors of those cells are lower than usual for they were children's doors. To the outsider walking through this wing there is a terrible feeling of the past and the suffering and hopelessness that at one time must have saturated the very walls of the place. Because of the overcrowding of the prisons today, such wings must still be used for men, and a man in custody there cannot permit himself to dwell on old tragedies, but must rather derive what humour he can at the expense of many forgetful officers and visitors who inadvertently strike their heads or knock their hats off on the cell doors.

Young people today do not go to prison; other means have been devised for their care in custody and their training through the system of Detention Centres, Approved Schools and Borstal Institutions. It is rare for anyone under the age of twenty-one to appear in a prison except on remand, and only where, because of the violent or unstable nature of that particular young person, no other place of safety can be found.

So far as possible star prisoners who are new offenders serving their first prison sentence are separated so that they may not be contaminated by association with older and more experienced 'crooks'. In this age of violence and wanton destruction of property often carried out by the young there may well be those who question the rightness of that reason, but rules have to be made to be best for the majority and it is obvious that it is right to take what steps are possible to prevent new offenders from mixing with hardened criminals.

Most cities have local gaols, and these contain prisoners of all varieties. There are men waiting for trial who are remanded in custody, first offenders, debtors or civil prisoners and men beginning long sentences, waiting to be transferred to prisons specially designed for that purpose. There are short sentence men from the Magistrates'

Courts serving one to six months, and for them it is as yet almost impossible to find staff and accommodation for training in useful trades or in adjustment for release.

It is one of the greatest problems at present that the overcrowding in our prisons is such that in most local gaols men are sharing three in a cell because the rise in serious crime has far outstripped the programme for new buildings. Work is found for as many hours of the day as possible, and evening classes are available for some. There are the usual contacts with chaplains, welfare officers and others, but in the main this group of short term prisoners do not get much in the way of pre-release training at present.

One way has become open in recent years which has greatly helped the congestion in local prisons, and particularly those men and women serving shorter sentences, so that they can live more normally and therefore find the transfer from custody to freedom less difficult, and this is the open prison. There are now many of these both for men and women, and because there are no walls and no fences round them these prisoners have to take the responsibility for their own behaviour and so do not lose the ability to manage their own affairs. At first these prisons were entirely for first offenders, but since the result of the experiment has proved to be good it has recently been decided to extend the experiment to quite a number who have served previous sentences.

There is an important point here for members of the public. Many people outside prison view with alarm the institution of open prisons, and some have regarded it as dangerous. Men who have served sentences for crimes, even serious crimes, all eventually come out. In the past these men have often left closed prisons without rehabilitation of any sort, and are amongst us today. Is it not infinitely better that wherever possible such men should have the benefit of some training under more natural conditions so that when they do come out they are less likely to go back to their old ways? Is this not a better protection to the public?

Another form of classification of recent years has been the establishment of preventive detention. This was designed to cope with the persistent offender, so that very long sentences of seven to fourteen years could be given to people over the age of thirty who had committed not less than three serious crimes for which prison sentences had been imposed. Such men serve the first year in their local gaols, under the usual hard conditions, and then are transferred to a preventive detention prison where they live rather differently from ordinary short term prisoners, having separate cells, and far more training opportunities in trades which should help them on release. The final stage of preventive detention has been that certain selected men are chosen for the hostel scheme whereby they still live inside the prison, but go outside to work at ordinary jobs in the local area during the day. Even this form of prison treatment has not proved entirely satisfactory. Some changes have already been made and others are under review.

Hostels have also become part of the rehabilitative training for other long term prisoners, and although they are still a fairly new form of training, and very limited in the numbers they can help, the idea is a splendid one and later developments will undoubtedly come that will make it possible for more men to have this opportunity.

The idea is that certain selected men, about twelve to twenty according to the size of the hostel, are allowed to live separately from other prisoners, going out to work each day at ordinary jobs in the neighbourhood. Their pay is given in to the prison and from it their board is paid and the money for their dependent families. The hostel men are allowed pocket money, and after their evening meal can go out for limited periods like ordinary people in the city where the hostel is situated. Any money left after their commitments have been met is saved for them on release, and this gives many men the chance to start with something when they are returned to freedom. Weekend visits home are allowed, and the hostels themselves are equipped with dining room, sitting room with television and other amenities. Many men start in jobs which they continue to work in after release, and they make outside friends, all of which helps them to start again.

Undoubtedly this is one of the best things which has been done in recent years, and employers up and down the country have co-operated with the prison authorities in providing suitable work and helping prisoners to get on their feet. People are beginning to realize the need to help ex-prisoners, as in many respects they resemble handicapped people, who need some extra care in the early days. Like all new things, the hostel scheme is going through many growing pains, and much has yet to be done. It was bound to be limited in the early days to the few, and this of course has occasioned much dissatisfaction amongst those who have not been selected, but in time there will be opportunities for extending it to many more.

Men serving preventive detention who do not make the hostel scheme have to be helped in other ways. Certain parts of such prisons are set aside for those nearing the end of their sentences so that they can go outside the prison with an escorting officer to become used to traffic and crowds of people. Sometimes they are taken to a football match or to a cinema, because the fear of people is a very real one for long term men. This also has proved to be a good thing, and the men who go out in this way wear their ordinary civvy clothes and are therefore not obvious to others. However, there is quite a lot of dissatisfaction when men on this section meet others who got the hostel scheme, and they seem quite unable to accept the fact that certain people were selected and not others.

It may be that in the future there will be whole prisons which will be hostels, but this will depend on the possibility of employment for far larger numbers of men and women outside in industry. Most prisoners agree that the hostel scheme is a good one, and many say that it is the best thing that has been done so far, in spite of all its faults and limitations.

Leave is granted during the last few months of sentence to all with two years and over in other than local prisons in order that they may visit their families and make useful contacts with employers about work on release. Not all prisoners have families or homes to visit in this way, and to counteract this various people have offered to take in prisoners who are homeless and see that they do not miss this opportunity. Such homes are inspected by the local probation officers as to their suitability before being accepted. The prisoner comes for one week during the last three months prior to his release. Many more could take part in this scheme if there were more people willing to open their homes. An important thing is that the prisoner should go to the kind of home he will fit into, and which is not too far removed from the background from which he has come, otherwise it is an embarrassment to the prisoner as to the family who entertains him, but the idea is growing and is doing good work in a rather limited field. Where it is a success the prisoner has friends to whom he can turn after release.

Splendid work is being done by the members of the probation service. These men and women, with their special training and their dedication to the work of rehabilitation, have been of untold help to many who have had the advantage of their friendship through the difficult months after release. Unfortunately there are not nearly enough of such people, and those who do this work often have big case loads and work many hours longer than most people know. It is not easy to find men and women who will undertake such arduous and often disappointing work and yet keep on doing all that they can for the prisoners in their care. Many ex-prisoners have shared this great benefit and appreciate the help they have received.

In the old days the Discharged Prisoners' Aid Association was well known to the public though possibly not the whole of the work they undertook. Many men have been helped in this way with friendship, clothes and sometimes money. Perhaps one of the best things they have done in recent years is the provision of welfare officers for the prisons, as was mentioned in an earlier chapter.

All kinds of experiments are being tried in different kinds of prisons towards help with release. In some, group therapy is being used to help prisoners to talk out some of their personal difficulties and although this was originally done by the medical profession only, now prison officers are being trained to take part, and as the experiment is fairly recent it may well be that in a few years time this will prove to be something so useful that it will be introduced much more widely.

The house system which is so great a part of the training in public schools, and also in corrective institutions for young people, is now being tried in certain prisons with very good results. In these institutions the personal influence of carefully selected officers plays a major part in rehabilitation.

Working towards a better adjustment on release, there are courses run under the name of Pre-Release in a great many prisons. All long term prisons have them and quite a number where men and women are serving shorter sentences. Attendance at the course is voluntary on the part of the prisoners because it is felt that in this way the best results can be achieved. If a man chooses to attend such a course he is more likely to respond than if he is ordered to go. Unfortunately this means that certain men who very greatly need to attend do not choose to go. It may be that a man feels he will lose face with his group of friends if he admits by attending that he thinks he needs help. It may also be that he likes to exercise his right of choice by staying away, or indeed he may be so anti-social that he would scorn anything done for his ultimate reclamation.

This is one of the problems of the courses, and it may be that in future some way will be found which will ensure that all men attend and share the benefits.

These courses cover many sides of life outside prison. In one open prison where there are men serving the final stages of extremely long sentences, groups of about twelve men are taken out of prison life for three days, during which they have an intensive course which includes visits to the nearest city and a practical introduction to the social services provided.

In general the subjects covered fall into four groups. One of these is concerned with employment and trade union membership, and is most necessary for all men, particularly those who have been out of circulation for a long time.

Another is concerned with the welfare services available, and particularly the probation service, so that all prisoners may know where and how they can get help after release.

More recently has come the introduction of discussion on 'Family Relations'. This vital subject is concerned with a prisoner's return to his family and his girl friend. Personal relationships are often difficult and were probably not easy before the prisoner was sentenced. During his absence his wife has had to carry on the home and manage the children alone, and there are personal difficulties of adjustment, including sexual relationship, fear of pregnancy and maladjustment which need thought and help. Such courses have brought out all sorts of problems in the discussion which have pointed to the need for help in this direction.

More recently still has come the introduction of discussion on money matters, and the perils and pitfalls of the hire purchase system. Discussion on tax and other financial matters has proved of the utmost help to men leaving prison even after short terms, for so many of them have little or no idea how to plan the budget. Another point in this course is that prisoners have had no responsibility during their time in custody, and are apt to regard a pay packet as pocket money to be spent on themselves for luxuries. Long term men have not had to think of the cost of food or billets and of clothing. Great ignorance has been found to exist amongst prisoners of the pitfalls of hire purchase agreements, and they have shown readiness to discuss this and learn.

Towards help after release, other organisations as well as the Statutory ones, such as the Probation service make contacts with prisoners before they leave the prison, and there are many of these Religious organisations. The YMCA, Toc H, the WVS, the New Bridge, and others, all play their part and there is no doubt whatever that if a man or woman has a mind to change the old way of life and make a fresh start there are ample opportunities. The difficulty is that all these things are available but that so few are really determined to take the friendship thus offered and use it the right way.

This is natural, because after all much of it seems like charity, and any man or woman recoils from that. On the other hand the 'spongers' are only too ready to take all they can get and are really laughing all the time, feeling that society owes them something for having sent them away for months or years.

The intention of so many people of goodwill outside the prison is most certainly there to help, but so often the right approach has not been made.

In all pre-release work one must reckon with the attitude of handicapped people and the things that mitigate against acceptance of much that is offered.

Perhaps it will be a help here to try and look at all this pre-release help through the eyes of prisoners themselves, and then it may be possible to find a better way of making such help acceptable.

Most prisoners at heart are not pleased with themselves for being inside. They know they are failures to some extent or they wouldn't have been caught in the first place, and when one has failed to achieve complete success one is naturally sore about it, although one doesn't admit this openly. To be seen in prison is to be seen as a failure and therefore it is natural to regard any good people coming along with offers of help as righteous and self-satisfied successes themselves, seeking to offer some sort of charity to people on a lower level.

No one likes to feel inferior and in the position of being unable to give anything in return. This starts things off on the wrong foot. From the angle of the do-gooders, so many people feel as though they are doing something voluntarily for rather inferior types who ought to be grateful for what they are offered. This is never said in so many words, but the attitude is there and is resented.

Outside people so often expect gratitude from prisoners for any help offered, and this they rarely get. It is not because prisoners are ungrateful, but because to be in a position of having to express gratitude all the time and having nothing to give in return is to be always in the wrong. This does not foster self-respect which is the one thing people in custody must have before they can make a success of their lives.

Obviously help must be given, and must be received, but it can only be accepted if it is given in the right way, so those who work with prisoners must realize this and as they are, for the time being, in the better position it is for them to change their approach to make it more acceptable.

Experiments recently made in the pre-release courses have shown that much can be done by altering the form. The room should not be set out like a school, with prisoners sitting in rows waiting to hear the lecture and having to put up their hands to speak, then marching back to their cells or billets, having taken little or no part in the proceedings. The best results are obtained where there is an easy atmosphere and the group, however large, sit at ease—perhaps in a circle—and are able to smoke if they wish. If the pre-release lecturer also sits the subject can be introduced and then opened to discussion so that everybody takes part.

An example of some of the things which come out in discussion can be given to illustrate how valuable it can be.

Take the case of the wife of a prisoner who has four small children. When her man is sentenced and the farewells have been said she goes home from the Court alone and worried by the burdens she has to face. Where will the money come from to manage? How do I get my money from the National Assistance? Can I visit my husband? Where will the bus fare come from when I visit him? Do I write? After the first misery is over she begins to feel hardly done by and her thoughts often go on these lines.

'It's all very well for him, he's all right. He hasn't got to worry where his next meal's coming from. How am I going to pay the hire purchase? He's all right, eating his head off in that place and clothes provided, but what about us? He ought to have thought of that before he did it—that's men for you,'—and so on. Resentment follows quickly and the future looks black indeed. The man inside waits for a letter that doesn't come and his imagination begins to work. 'She's all right—she's outside and free. Why couldn't she have written? It's not much to expect, is it? There must be another man.' A situation is building up both sides. Later on when the pattern of separation is established and the wife getting her National Assistance money and managing as best she can she probably needs some help with things in the house. Not all women can mend fuses or repair sinks and mend the structure of the place. This means that neighbours have to be brought in and perhaps the man next door fixes the fuse or puts up a shelf for her. The husband in prison thinks about this when he hears that old Bill Bloggs next door has been going into his house, and because the husband is alone and has a lot of time to think he imagines that Bill Bloggs is taking the opportunity of his absence from home by having an affair with the wife. The prisoner rarely thinks it is his fault for having got into trouble, and having let the wife down. He is trying to build up his own ego by blaming someone else, so he plans what he will do when he comes out.

Near the time of his release he may notice a change in the wife's attitude. Maybe she has visited regularly and even written quite affectionately, but then she seems cold and this confirms his suspicions. Actually what has probably happened is that the wife has suddenly realized that he is coming home and that she may become pregnant again. If he then gets into more trouble what will she do? She's had four children to cope with this time, and how could she face it again with five?

Discussion on family relations often leads to much necessary information being given to prisoners about family planning and it is hoped that during the rest of the time before he leaves on release he will try to think over the things that have been discussed a bit more sensibly and understandingly about the problems that the family outside have had to face. Such talks have often resulted in men seeking useful information from probation officers and from marriage guidance counsellors as well as from other organizations in the social services.

Ideas for the best line of action in any difficulty are often brought forward by the group, and it is helpful if this is so because the men listen to what the others say and it is easier to accept ideas from other men than from outsiders.

Another problem for those who have children is that the man in prison so often forgets that the children have grown up quite a lot during the time he has been away. Ron goes home to his wife and family after thinking about his little five-year-old son Peter, and imagining how he will pick him up and hug him, give him sweets and receive the affection he has so sadly missed whilst he has been away. Peter meanwhile is now eight years old. He has been, in his own childish opinion, the 'man' of the house whilst his Dad was in prison. He resents being picked up and cuddled as though he were still a baby, and anyway father is a stranger at first because three years is a long time in his little life. Ron realizes that the boy is pushing him off and his first reaction is 'The wife's been turning him away from me.' The group will see this situation and always have a number of ideas as to how best Ron can win back the affection of little Peter.

Frequently the group ask 'Should we tell the children where we have been?' The ensuing discussion always brings out some very important facts that the children find out if they are not told, and that children are extremely loyal and can accept such situations if the parents put it to them in the right way.

These and many other subjects are discussed, and all the factors about future employment, telling the employer about past prison sentences, getting accommodation, learning to save, avoiding the traps of people selling things at the door and offering 'something for nothing', or almost nothing.

Pre-release courses come in the last six months of long sentences so that the people in prison still have a little time to think over what has been said and to talk to each other about the ideas that have been brought out.

It is good to know how much is being done during the sentence towards rehabilitation, but it is not nearly enough yet. More help of the right kind is needed so that some of the suspicion and anti-social feelings can be broken down.

In spite of all the help that is being given, there are still those men and women who have not availed themselves of any chance provided. It is about these men that we must think next.

We will now trace the story of George as he leaves prison and try to see the first few days from his eyes. We will examine his feelings and the kind of help he may expect to receive and see how he gets on.

I have chosen for this story a man who has served a sentence of four years. His problems will be those of a fairly long-sentence man but in varying degrees they are the usual problems of most men and women leaving prison. He will be an average sort of prisoner, of ordinary educational standards, and with no home. He will not have been a particularly responsive prisoner, and he will have had his difficulties inside. He has refused pre-release help.

F

5

COMING OUT

(As described and felt by an ex-prisoner)

George couldn't sleep. He tossed and turned on his narrow bed, trying to find a new position which would help him to doze off. Why couldn't he sleep? Maybe he was missing the others who used to share his cell before this pre-release business. Took a bit of getting used to being on your own again. Perhaps it was the silence. Missed old Tom's snoring, maybe. Of course there were the usual prison noises going on just the same. Old Timson's round tonight. Why couldn't the *screw* realize that people were trying to get to sleep—banging all the ruddy doors and making as much noise as a dozen screws. Waiting for the next round, that's what it was. Somehow you can't sleep when you know you're waiting—waiting for the next round, waiting to know which of them will be coming.

Four long dreary years he'd been here, all except those first few months in the local *nick*—Four years without a decent bed to sleep in and every night shut up in the cell with your thoughts and the other chaps. Bob wasn't so bad—he'd like to see him again outside, but that Syd! Ruddy old sex maniac, that's what he was. All that talk— women all the time. Oh well, that was over now, but all the same it was different being by yourself again these last few weeks. Hadn't thought much those first years, but now—two more weeks and three days—no, only two now because it was another day already. The light was beginning to show in the square of window. Wonder what it'll be like to look out of a window without bars for a change? Rain lashed the window, in a sudden gust, and a draught blew the picture over on the shelf. Bess—that was the picture. She'd been a bit of all right had Bess. Wonder where she is now? Oh well, there'd be others—all the same—a chap was fine when he could pay for them. Some chaps were lucky, had wives who came to visit them, and kids too. 'Good job I haven't any,' he thought—'shan't have that problem.'

Two weeks and two days and then—wonder where I'll be sleeping that night? Got to get some money before I can sleep any place.

George lay thinking about that problem. Four years is a long time, a chap forgets. 'Wonder if I can still do a *job*? I'll have to do one pretty quickly if I'm going to live. Of course—parson's still on about going straight and making money honest. Lot he knows about it. Got to have some money before you can go honest anyway, and where the hell does he think I'm going to get it from?'

George turned over again and finally gave up all attempt to get to sleep. The Welfare officer came to mind—'Suppose I could have asked him to fix something up? Well, I've *done my bird* without asking any old B for anything and I'm not going to start now. I managed before and I'll manage again.' George ran his fingers through his hair and tried to rub out the tight feeling that had been there every night lately. He felt screwed up, that throbbing feeling, as if his head was going to burst. These long nights. They used not to be like that.

'Can't sleep nowadays,' he said to Bill when they began work next day. ' "Gate fever," that's what you've got, you old sod. Won't go now till you get out.'

'Doesn't seem like the time will ever pass. Funny that,

when you come to think of it. For years I've not bothered about time—it's just gone by one way or another, but now—it's like hearing a clock tick-ticking inside you, ticking the time away until something happens.'

George noticed other things, too. He didn't fancy his food, and although he usually had a good appetite and finished up his plate he couldn't seem to fancy it any more. Probably the sleepless nights had something to do with it.

Standing in the Governor's office a few days later he found he was nervous. The floor didn't seem quite straight. 'Stand up and take you hands out of your pockets, Brown.' Robinson gave him a glare in the eye. George looked daggers. He hated Robinson, always had—the man seemed to have had a down on him from the first, but he stood up and tried not to behave too badly for after all, if Robinson *nicked* him now he might lose the last of his *remission* and he might not get out on the 25th after all.

'Have you seen anyone about a job yet, Brown?' asked the Governor.

'Not yet, sir.'

'Why not? You'll have to find something to do—the Government won't keep you once you're out, you know.'

'I've got a cousin in the town who said he'd help me get something, sir—something in the painting and decorating,' lied George, rather than say nothing.

'Well, mind you get to work as soon as you can. You've got to help yourself now.'

'Yes sir, yes, I know sir—my cousin will fix me up.'

'Why don't you have a word with Mr Fawcett, the Welfare Officer, Brown? He might be able to help you.'

'Yes, sir'—but George didn't go. He didn't want help. He wanted to be rid of the whole bally lot of them and find his own way round.

There was the problem about clothes. He'd chosen a dark suit from the store—and a sleeveless pullover. That suit wouldn't show up like a sports jacket, and George didn't want to have people looking at him. Days and nights dragged by. Some of his old pals seemed to keep out of his way, and Bert—who hadn't spoken to him for months—kept on trying to get him to take a message to his missus when he got out. 'There'll be some money for you if you go there,' he kept saying.

Well, he wasn't going there. Bert always had a lot of ideas and they never came to anything. Like as not he'd go to the address and they'd have left. Wasn't going to waste his first day out looking up Bert's people and asking them to send him some *snout*. 'Get something,' would he? Bert would 'get something' if he didn't leave him alone.

Lying awake on his last night George felt sick. He was alone now, eating his supper—the food stuck in his throat. He was alone now, he wouldn't see the others again. His clothes were there—the new clothes he'd put on in the morning when the others had gone. He'd miss some of them—'Wish Paddy was going out with me,' he thought. 'Wouldn't be so bad if you had a buddy to go with.' If only the lie he'd told about the cousin had been true it wouldn't have been so bad. He really would like to know he was going to get a job and have somewhere to stay. Perhaps he ought to have chosen the sports suit—the trouble was he didn't really know what it was like now outside. He thought how everyone would look at him and stare if his suit didn't look like everyone else's. He was hungry now and it was too late—'Wish I'd got a mug of hot tea inside me,'—he thought what a fool he'd been not to eat when he could have.

Next morning he'd lost his appetite again and that sick feeling was back. 'Feels funny wearing all these new things,' he thought. 'I'll look silly walking about the town in that—ought to have something old that people wouldn't notice.'

When his cell door was opened for the last time he felt
cold in his new clothes. The mackintosh was thin, and the
suit wasn't as warm as the one he'd got used to wearing.
His hands fumbled with the tie, and the collar of the
shirt with the tie felt tight and he couldn't breathe
properly. He'd cut himself shaving and that hadn't
helped. His hand wasn't as steady as it usually was.
'What the hell is the matter with me?' he thought.

At the gate there was a good fire in the officers' room
and George would have liked to have stood near it and
warmed himself, but old Shorty was on duty this morning
and he'd have made some ribald joke if he had. Better
not try any tricks, the old b—— could keep me in if he
thought I was playing up—wish I could push his face in—
it would be my luck that old Shorty was on the gate.

George felt sick and hungry at the same time.

'Wait a minute—wait a minute—there's plenty of time
—what's all the hurry about, Brown?' said Shorty. 'I
don't like your face any more than I did when you came
here, and you'd better see that I don't ever set eyes on it
again.'

George clenched his hands in his pockets and swore
softly under his breath.

'What was that you said?' leered Shorty.

George had collected his five shillings, given to a man
on release, and at last the outer gate was opened. Rain,
that had been falling steadily since last night, was lashing
down, and he fastened up the mac as best he could. As he
stepped over the sill Shorty called out 'Have a nice time,
and we'll expect you back in a couple of days.'

George was out and free. The gate had shut behind him
after nearly four long years, and now he could do what he
liked. This was the moment for which he had been waiting,
and now here he was, cold, frightened, and alone.

He set off towards the centre of the city, stepping out

quickly, partly to keep warm and partly so that no one would see him anywhere near the prison gate. He wanted food and something hot inside him so he meant to find some café open and get inside out of the rain and relax. It was 7.45 a.m. and people were crowding along going to work and there were plenty of cars about and buses too.

Of course, George had forgotten that no eating place would be open, and so his walk round the town, vaguely remembered, ended in a fruitless search for hot tea.

No good going to the Labour Exchange at this time, it won't be open, he thought. How hateful it was walking about the streets like this. George sheltered in a doorway, watching the people and hoping they were not watching him, though he was sure they were. Even walking along there was that horrid feeling that someone was walking behind. Once he swung round sharply thinking he was being followed, but it was nothing and he relaxed with an oath muttered under his breath. By now he hated his prison mac, it was too long and too light and it didn't look like the coats other people were wearing. 'I'd get rid of it now if I'd got something else,' he thought.

About 9 a.m. he stumbled rather than walked into a café just opening. Chairs were still on the tables, and a weedy looking youth was sweeping out into the street. It took some time to get his cup of tea, but the welcome warmth raised his spirits a bit, and he bought some cheese rolls too—left over from the day before but he was hungry and they tasted good anyway. He bought a packet of fags, and then realized that most of the 5s od had gone. This decided him to visit the National Assistance place first, and after some difficulty he found the way. It was sheer hell asking people the way. George couldn't get over the feeling that he was being watched, and once—from habit —he said 'Sir' to a man who looked very surprised, and again George shrunk a little inside his chilly mac. 'Good

God,' he thought, 'a chap can't even speak without giving away that he's not like other people.'

The National Assistance office was not open until 10 o'clock and it meant standing about outside. Soon the packet of fags was almost empty, and he'd no money for more. 'Oh well, I'll get some soon in this place,' he thought. Inside there were rows of benches on which already a motley group of people were collecting, waiting to see the various officials in the little counter boxes. George was called quite quickly and his hopes rose, but it was only to give his particulars and then he was told to wait on the benches and he'd be called again.

Wet and miserable he sat down, feeling frustrated, watching the various types who came along. There were the wives, some with babies and small children, people who often came here and were quite used to waiting. Some of the children played about and some ate food their mothers had brought to help while away the time. There were men, too—scruffy types some of them, longish hair and dirty suede shoes. 'Bet some of them have never done a day's work in their lives,' he thought.

There were older men, some of them looking almost as embarrassed as George himself, and sitting patiently looking down at the floor, huddled in their coats. George began to speculate about these. 'Bet they hate it having to come here—like begging for charity—God! I'll never come to these places again—if this is going honest I can do better *screwing*—What a life!'

It was almost noon before the call came to George and he found himself seated before an official with a long sheet of paper on which many particulars had to be written. 'Wish the sod would keep his ruddy voice down,' thought George as he answered the questions, fearfully hoping the chaps standing near couldn't hear what was being said. 'Have you been to the Labour Exchange yet?' asked the official. He hadn't, and he soon learned that he must go there first before any money would be forthcoming.

Footsore from walking on the unaccustomed pavements George set out again, only to find another long line was waiting and again he must queue for his place. There was work, it seemed, work of a kind on the roads and he could start on Monday. 'Monday,' he thought, 'and today it's Friday. How the hell do they think I'm going to live until then on nothing?' Then there would be a week in hand with his pay and in fact he'd got to live until the end of the next week before he'd see any money.

Back to the National Assistance office and another long wait produced 30s with the information that he could come back again next week to get some more.

'Like hell I will,' he thought angrily. How could he live on 30s. The man had asked him where he was staying and he didn't know, so they couldn't give him anything until he knew how much it would be.

'Free, am I?' he thought, 'Free as ruddy air, and I get meself a place to stay and feed meself and go to work on Monday all on 30s and then I can go back and crawl round for more—not ruddy likely.' The 30s bought a really good meal and some drinks and smokes. 'No use saving it—I might as well enjoy myself whilst I can. Perhaps I ought to have asked Mr Fawcett to help me, or the chaplain, perhaps that's how they get even with you if you don't ask for help, so you'll have no money and nowhere to stay and then you'll have to crawl around begging.' Out in the street he remembered the Discharged Prisoners' Aid Society he'd heard about and he hadn't meant to go there, but it seemed as if he must do something. He knew where it was because the chaps inside had told him, but it took some finding and it was nearly 4 o'clock before he got there. No one seemed to be about, and presently he saw a notice outside giving opening hours. It seemed that the office would have been open in the morning but it was closed now until the next day.

The rain had stopped by now, but it was still cold and dull, and George counted the last of his 30s. 'Might as well go and see a flick,' he thought, 'at least I'd be able to sit down, and when it's dark I'll see what I can pick up.'

Four hours later, when he'd had a good sleep in the warmth of the cinema, George once more emerged into the street—this time with more confidence for it was dark and the bright lights of the shop windows and street lamps made him feel good. His feet were still tired and he soon found his way into a down-town pub that he'd heard about inside, and there with his mug of beer amongst the noisy motley crowd beginning the evening's merry-making he took stock of his position. Sixpence half-penny left of the 30s, no prospect of a bed, only the doss house, no prospect of another meal and nobody to talk to.

'Hi! If it isn't old George,' said a friendly voice all of a sudden, and there, coming across from the bar, was 'Mug-face', who had been with him in the first year in the local gaol. Was George glad to see him! 'Hi, two more of the best,' called 'Mug-face', and soon they were talking at a small table in a corner.

'When did you come out, George?'

'Just come.'

'What's on?'

'Ruddy nothing.'

In a few words George outlined his first day's search for money and work.

'Say, you ruddy fool, you don't want to do that! Who wants their stinking money? There's plenty to be picked up here in——. Look at me now, nice job of it I'd have made if I'd tried to play their ruddy game, wouldn't I?'

Looking round carefully to see that they were not over-heard there followed a short talk very much to the point, and later, after a few more drinks paid for by 'Mug-face', the two left together.

George didn't turn up at the job on Monday morning. He had no need to. He was in funds, thanks to 'Mug-face', and what if he were 'on the run' again? What the hell anyway?

George is out. He is one of many whose experience of release from prison has followed a similar pattern. Let us now look at some of the comments so often made by people on the right side of the fence who have little understanding of the problems of release.

'What a fool the man was!'

'Why didn't he ask the welfare officer, or the chaplain, to help him get work?'

'The man could have told the truth in the first place and something would have been done for him.'

'But we know there are people at the Labour Exchange who deal especially with cases of men coming out of prison, and if he'd asked about it he'd have had help.'

'What are the chaplains and welfare officers for except to help men get a good start?'

'Anyone could have told him where the local D.P.A. office was, and when it was open. They'd even have made an appointment for him.'

'Five shillings was quite enough to last him until he could get help.'

'He was jolly lucky anyway to be given five shillings after what he'd done.'

'Why should he expect to steal and rob decent people and then imagine they're going to make life easy for him when he comes out?'

'It's hard enough for ordinary honest people to get a job and accommodation without bending over backwards to help felons!'

'Let him suffer! He's asked for it. Why should special arrangements be made for people who never thought about anyone but themselves anyway?'

. . . and so on.

These are not imaginary remarks. All of them have been said many times by people who speak first and think afterwards.

The fact remains that George—who probably never did think of anyone but himself, and who has robbed his fellow men and didn't use any common sense, has come out. He is here amongst us, and if he doesn't make good who will suffer? George? Yes, in time he will get caught and go back, but before he does he will have robbed someone else. The tax-payers will again have to keep him in prison for a few more years, so that little will have been achieved by all that righteous indignation.

In actual fact, George—because of his past life and the reason that for many years he has been a number and not a proper man—was not likely to make good and do the sensible thing on release.

The 'George' who left prison that morning was neither sensible nor clever. He was immature, frightened, and alone for all his bravado. Greatly in need of help, but quite unable to admit it, George hadn't a chance to do well in a strange world where he had never done an ordinary honest job. Life is hard enough at times for people who have kept on the right side of the law, and have followed some honest occupation. Nobody likes to ask for help, yet most of us, if we are truthful, must admit times when this has been necessary. Ordinary people can recall occasions when they have been only too thankful to accept the help of a friend in some difficulty, but a prisoner does not see things as we do.

Years without liberty make him over-anxious to exercise his independence, so that although he knows that there are people who would be willing to assist him, he doesn't want to ask because that makes him feel inferior.

I have talked to many men about this. One man tried to analyse his feelings about accepting help. He was an old lag, with many prison years behind him.

'It's like this,' he told me. 'People always want to drag up the past. I've done my *bird* and it's finished. I'm free now and I've got a lot of lost time to make up. All these people who say they want to help are just giving you charity. I've had enough of that sort of thing—it puts you in the wrong anyway. I want to do as I like now—be the same as anyone else. I've had enough of being pushed around. When people help you they think they've got the right to tell you what to do and you're lucky to have them helping you—'spose they get some sort of kick out of it—makes them feel "I'm better than you", sort of thing! Us chaps don't see it like that. We've done our punishment and now we want to have some of the things we've missed. Half the do-gooders that help you turn nasty if you don't go and do exactly what they say—gives them a feeling of power, ordering us chaps around, and we've had enough of that while we've been inside.'

That is the real problem of after-care.

How can we help a man who needs help but doesn't want it?

Hundreds of men and women of good will are anxious to do what they can to help and reform ex-prisoners, but they want to do it their way. They expect the ex-prisoner to admit that he is wrong and to be grateful for what is being done for him. If he will adopt an attitude of humility they will give him good advice, perhaps even money to help, but always he must make it quite clear that he is inferior and indeed very lucky that other folk are condescending to help him at all.

If a prisoner were a sensible mature person, able to see

his way of life was wrong, and that all he had to do on release was to avail himself of the help extended to him through the many agencies of social service, no doubt his rehabilitation would be almost automatic. He would ask for assistance, go to the right place, accept the help that was offered, wouldn't waste the money from the National Assistance Board on drink and smoking, but carefully use it so that it lasted all the week. He would be found a job, go every day, work hard and remember to thank his benefactors, who would be delighted with themselves for having done such a grand job!

If prisoners were sensible hard-working grateful people, and careful over money, they wouldn't be ex-prisoners. They'd be ordinary honest men and women who never got into trouble and there'd be no need for after-care. In fact, they'd be paragons of virtue and a lot better than most of us.

If after-care is to be more successful in future some serious thinking must be done, and a new approach found.

As has been said, there are many organizations doing fine work at present. Men who have served periods of Corrective Training and Preventive Detention become subject to licence and after-care supervision upon release from prison, also men serving life sentences.

In the past the Probation Officer acted as an associate for the Central After-Care Association and before the man's release a great deal of provision was made for his reception at home. In many cases, of course, where the man had no relatives and no where to go, accommodation was found and quite frequently the man was met upon his arrival in the area by his Associate and taken to the new lodgings which had been reserved for him. Many of the initial difficulties of rehabilitation had already been ironed out before the man was released, and often employment was waiting for him with a sympathetic employer,

who was well aware of the man's past and willing to give
him a chance to prove his worth and to help him toward
re-establishment in the community.

It has been possible for men who have served long prison
sentences, four years and over, or three years from central
prisons, to volunteer for after-care under Probation
Officers, and although these cases, as far as the Probation
Officer is concerned, are termed 'voluntary', the same
amount of work, care and consideration is given to them
and there is little doubt that many men who might otherwise have floundered shortly after their release have found
a friend to help them through the difficult stages toward
a useful and purposeful life.

Men who have served preventive detention and corrective training are only a fraction of the number of
releases from prison each year, and there is still much to
be done for those men who serve shorter sentences and
who find themselves outside the prison gates, often not
knowing where to go for the next meal or where, in fact,
they will find shelter that particular night. At present
these men have been considerably helped by the Discharged Prisoners' Aid Society, also by Prison Welfare
Officers, who go to extraordinary lengths to make plans
for these men upon release, but so often without the assistance of an outside Associate they find themselves frustrated, rejected and depressed by the first experiences of
freedom, often resort to crimes and face yet again, another
prison sentence.

New arrangements are being made to make it possible
for any ex-prisoner to obtain help through the Probation
service since the report on the treatment of offenders, also
for payment of National Assistance money on release for
certain cases.

In recent years a splendid piece of work has been
started under the Norman House Scheme, which provides

in each of its centres a real home for certain small groups of homeless ex-prisoners.

The difficulty seems to be that all these after-care organizations cater for such small numbers at so great a cost, and each seems to work in its own particular field.

There has been a tendency in the past to select carefully those ex-prisoners who are most likely to make good, avoiding all sex-offenders, or men with records for crimes of violence. The reason put forward is a very real one, that the public would soon be alarmed and would frustrate attempts to house and care for such people in residential areas.

This has always seemed to be so short-sighted, because if the greatest danger to the public comes from criminals with records for violence and sex-crimes, then surely it is better to concentrate on these offenders more than any others, and to take special care to do everything possible to rehabilitate them. It is not the fault of after-care organizations that this is not being done, but rather the lack of understanding on the part of the public. As things stand today it is these difficult ex-prisoners who get the least after-care and therefore they come out of prison continually forming a hard core of recedivism and danger. These men need the hostel scheme, the open prison, the after-care of probation officers and other agencies as well as residential care sometimes. Unfortunately people not appreciating the true facts often make this impossible by horror and outcry if such people are known to be around.

This reminds me of an amusing story. Some long sentence men were recently transferred from closed to open conditions where previously there were only *stars*, or first offenders. The attitude of the star prisoners on the arrival of the long-term men was surprisingly the same as that of the public—'We shall all be murdered in our beds!' No such violence occurred and in time everybody settled down to ordinary co-existence.

Robert was interviewed in a closed prison with a view to providing an opportunity of rehabilitation in an open institution. On examination of his record, which extended over most of his adult life, there came to light the fact that fifteen years ago he had offered violence to the night watchman in a factory where he intended to rob a safe. Some risk might have been involved had Robert been given this opportunity of rehabilitation in open conditions, and failure would have brought to light his previous crimes. Public outrage follows such reports in the press, so the greater risk was taken about which the public knew nothing—of permitting Robert to finish his imprisonment inside and leave in the ordinary way at the completion of his sentence. Robert is not yet free, but one day he will be, and because he is a frustrated man he will be a greater danger than ever.

Adverse public opinion is the reason why so many attempts at rehabilitation move so slowly. Those in authority are courageous and far-seeing men and women, but they know that there will be failures whatever efforts are made. These failures will be widely publicised and may jeopardize the whole experiment, so of necessity they have to be selective.

The problem of crime will always be with us, but of recent years this has grown so alarmingly that every citizen is appalled. Outbreaks of violence and of wholesale destruction and hooliganism have spot-lighted the whole system of justice in our country and others. Something must be done to reduce the present numbers in our prisons and borstals and ways must be found to train, re-educate and re-direct the minds of those who are outside the law.

Another difficulty which has not so far been mentioned

G

is the old lag's attitude towards the victims of his crimes. Many old lags are my very good friends, and I have discussed this with them on numerous occasions. Many of them are kindly, friendly people in ordinary life, with a great loyalty to those who have befriended them.

I remember John many years ago, during the war, who was a regular member of a club. Usually no member of the club ever stole anything—the property of the club was regarded as sacred, nor would anyone have stolen furniture, soap, towels, or other things. Suddenly the mirror in the men's toilet disappeared, and although this was replaced the second one also went. John was simply furious. He—a burglar of many years himself—allowed no one to steal from his place; that was outside his code. He never did find the culprit and it was a lasting annoyance to him that someone had 'pulled a fast one' on him!

Bert, another thief, once fell to the temptation very wrongly provided by someone who left large sums of money lying about in club premises. Bert had been a trusted member of the club until that time, and knew perfectly well where cigarettes and small sums of canteen money were to be found. One day the club was entered and a robbery took place which afterwards was found to be Bert's work. The large sum of money so wrongly left about by the very stupid helper was taken, but the cigarettes and small canteen float were not touched. The club itself was not robbed because Bert had a sense of loyalty to those who had befriended him.

I have known very few ex-prisoners who were so depraved as to rob their friends.

Freddy was one of these. Work was found for him in a nearby small business through the great kindness of an employer. After some weeks, in a sudden fit of villainy, Freddy helped himself to the till and *blew*. A letter of apology followed later because Freddy suddenly realized that in doing this he had really robbed his friends, for the money had to be made good. It would not be surprising if one day the debt were paid.

Freddy had also offended against his own kind, for no further help could be asked for an ex-prisoner in that particular employment, and others were thus deprived of an opportunity of work.

This case was an exception. In many years of placing men in employment social workers have met with the utmost kindness and consideration from employers to whom they and their friends the ex-prisoners would like to pay tribute, nor have these employers been let down. Even where men have failed, they have not failed the employer who had befriended them, nor closed the door for another prisoner to work in that particular place in future.

In spite of this loyalty, the men's attitude to the unknown victims of their crimes is a puzzling one.

'Ernie, why did you take that car?'

'Well, I couldn't buy one, could I?'

'No, but what about the poor man whose car it was—don't you ever think of him?'

'Well—he'd get another, he was insured, wasn't he?'

This seems to be a general idea that if one of 'them' has something and it is stolen 'they' have only got to claim insurance and all is well. The victim hasn't really lost anything, he'd only be without it for a short time, so why worry?

A good many people would like to think that being insured made things so easy!

Norman once had a great surprise. He had really made good and was working in a steady job, having resisted all temptation to go back to his old life. One day he had a serious accident which resulted in a broken limb. Since this was an insurance case he expected that very soon full compensation would be paid. In the end, after several months of considerable hardship, some money was recovered, but the time lag and the inconvenience and uncertainty provided an object lesson which might otherwise have failed to register.

People in general, their cars and property, are to many old lags fair game. If the house owner is a business man or in one of the professions, 'Oh well—he's got plenty more where that came from' is the usual attitude.

Driving in my car one day with an old lag, many years ago, certain houses were pointed out to me. 'There's money in that one,' and again 'He doesn't bank his money—it's all in the house, six or seven hundred each week-end.'

'How do you know?'

'We have to know—after all, it's our job, isn't it?'

The foolish member of the public who provides temptation in this way might well reflect on that little incident. Those whose job is crime have no sympathy for him. 'He asks for it and he gets it!'

'Doesn't it ever worry you that you may be caught and go down for a long sentence?' I have frequently asked old lags.

'Somehow that doesn't stop us,' I have been told by many. 'It's a bit like in war time. We knew that there was a danger of stopping a bullet—that made life exciting, but we never thought it would be our bullet, so we just went on.'

The excitement, the adventure, the considerable skill in planning and carrying out difficult jobs, appeals to some men, as big game hunting appeals to others more fortunately placed. Thinking of rehabilitation, we must remember the kind of work open to the average ex-prisoner who begins a new job when he is no longer young. He works in the same place day after day, never using the skill of which he has become a master—lonely, bored, and often friendless, it is easy to see the whole vast problem of those first few months after release.

Ordinary people have to learn to accept this boredom and monotony which is often characteristic of our industrial age, but we have the activities and hobbies of our leisure time, and our roots in home and family which create interest and provide opportunity for our imagination and skill. We have accepted that this is the way of life for most human beings today. Prisoners from another background have not accepted this, and it goes hard with them during the first few months after release. So far no answer has been found but more must be done to provide the opportunities for men to find useful outlets for their leisure time which will bring the rewards they so greatly need to help overcome this initial burden of keeping straight.

The need is for friendship to overcome loneliness, trust to stimulate a growing responsibility, personal interest to defeat boredom and tide over those difficult months until the consciousness of virtue brings its own reward.

This is not only the duty of the administrators of prisons, and the after-care organizations, but of every thinking man and woman. People must prepare to help, not only in the detection of crime, by assisting the police, but by accepting back into society those who have been punished and are yet unable to fend for themselves without some support.

Experiments are continually being tried but they need help from the public—far greater help than has yet been available.

For many years efforts have been made to find new ways of redirection for ex-prisoners during the first few difficult months after release. An outline of a plan which might assist hundreds of men and women may perhaps set people thinking.

In the chapters that follow is a description of an experiment in after-care which has been attempted and which has begun to fill this need in one area.

It might well be that other people could try something on similar lines, and a new approach be made.

6

AN EXPERIMENT IN AFTER-CARE

For many years a group of people had run a club for men
and women between the ages of 18–30 years in a large city.
Owing to the difficulties of financing such a scheme it had
been decided by the committee to try something entirely
new. Premises were acquired which had at one time been
a down-town public house, an old coaching inn, then
standing empty, awaiting demolition.

This property was rented from the local authority until
such time as the site was needed for town improvements.

An old coaching inn provides an ideal place for a club
since it has many small rooms as well as large cellars
which can be used as work shops. It also has residential
accommodation where a club leader can live.

The experiment consisted of using part of the premises
for a café run as an ordinary business during the day,
with a paid staff employed by the committee, and the
proceeds of the café were designed to pay the overhead
expenses so that the club could be run free of cost during
the evenings.

For eight years this club had been financed in this way,
with some additional help in the way of gifts of furniture
and occasional donations of money, the evening work
being carried out by a team of voluntary helpers.

In 1962 it was decided that the club was no longer
needed in that particular area, and it was closed down.

During the whole life time of the club, and for many

years before the café was opened, the committee had made it their policy to take a certain number of handicapped people such as ex-prisoners and ex-borstal men amongst the ordinary membership and it was such people who would suffer inevitably when the club closed down.

The value of the work done for these men and women had been considerable, and it was felt that some responsibility remained for them, as they would no longer have a place to go to in the evenings where the help and interest of friendly workers was always available.

One old lag in particular had felt very greatly the need to continue this kind of after-care, having benefited himself from the facilities provided, and was anxious to help others in the same way. After much discussion, a plan was formed to try the experiment of running an Old Lags' Association in the premises now vacated by the club, and the committee agreed to continue the café to provide an income.

Many people in other countries as well as in England have wondered about the advisability of allowing old lags to get together after their sentences have finished. Some countries strenuously oppose all attempts at providing places where this could happen, feeling that the less ex-prisoners see of each other the better. There is naturally the fear that gangs will form to commit further crimes.

On the side of the prisoners themselves there have often been comments that once they get out they do not want to have anything more to do with prisons and prisoners. 'We've had enough of them inside.'

There are good reasons for this point of view, but there are other factors that must be recognized.

First of all, if a man comes out of prison with the intention of going back to crime—possibly the only life he knows—then he will certainly do so, and will seek out and find others of like mind to help him, either as confederates or as *fences* to get rid of stolen property. Since prisoners look exactly like ordinary men and women it is difficult to know whether those men drinking their beer in the corner of the public house are plotting mischief or are perfectly respectable honest people. Anyone can go into a public house, and if their behaviour is correct nobody can object, and there are many public houses.

Members of the police force know well that certain licensed premises and also certain coffee houses and other centres of evening refreshment are used in this way by gangs, but so long as the behaviour of the patrons is correct nobody can stop this happening. Therefore ex-prisoners, if they wish, can certainly get in touch with each other.

Secondly, the old lag who wants to forget all about prisons and prisoners is going to be very lonely. If a man has been inside for many years it may well be that he has no outside contacts and a large number have no family connections nor friends. Such a man, if he intends to mix solely with those on the right side of the law, must avoid mentioning his past, and must constantly be on the watch to see that he does not give himself away by some chance remark or action.

Nobby was one of these. Careful, watchful and quick to learn, he managed to avoid detection for some time in a new group of men and women. One day he was discussing his old grandma who was failing in health and didn't like to go out alone. Said Nobby 'She always has an *escort* when she goes out.'

'An escort?' was the answer from one of the group. 'Is she mental?'

Nobby flushed. He'd slipped up rather badly. An escort or prison officer goes with a prisoner moving about the prison and is a word not used by people outside. The flush of annoyance was most damaging and Nobby slipped away as soon as possible.

The manner in which an old lag rolls his cigarette can betray him to those who know, for this is an art in which almost all old lags excel, for how else would the tobacco ration last out?

Keeping up appearances can be very tiring, and yet one must be careful not to dose off in a comfortable chair or a sudden noise or touch may spark off some reaction.

Newspapers can be, and are, read in prison, but the local gossip about topical events is often unknown to a man just out.

Only a short time ago Dave was talking about the fare to London. 'Of course, it's cheaper to get a return,' he observed to a group of people. Dave had only just come out after eight years.

'Cheaper to get a return?' said someone, laughing. 'Man, how long is it since you travelled by train?'

Dave was quick and covered up with a tale of having been everywhere by car for the last six or seven years, and he'd forgotten for the moment, but it gave him a nasty shock.

One can act a part for a certain time each day, but sometimes one gets exhausted and a man is glad enough to relax in the company of another who has shared the same past. Probably he has kept his mouth shut most of the time for fear of making just such a slip, and he longs to talk to someone.

Many people were consulted before the experiment of running the Old Lags' Association was started, including prison governors, chief constables, and probation officers. It was mentioned to the members of the then Prison Commission, and all were interested. Some were dubious, but the need for new kinds of after-care is so great that everyone felt the experiment worth trying.

It was agreed that great secrecy must be maintained in the early days, since ex-prisoners are so suspicious and would be unlikely to use the new club if it became the centre of attention in the city.

A carefully worded paragraph was put in the local papers, and the press co-operated magnificently, not publishing anything more than was required. Many attempts were made by reporters of national newspapers to find out about 'OLA', but editors were exceptionally kind when circumstances were explained, and the news was not permitted to leak out.

Small cards were prepared and given to welfare officers of the nearby prisons, and ex-prisoners who had already been members of the former club did much to spread the news on the *grape-vine*.

Eventually the opening day arrived, and none of the helpers knew quite what to expect. The club was to be open every night for the winter months, and an experimental period was fixed covering eight months. Curtains were provided for the café, so that full privacy would be maintained, and the inconspicuous side-entrance only was to be used. Helpers volunteered to come along and serve meals if necessary, and small rooms were provided with a hired television, radio and a record player.

The new venture was prepared for almost anything.

The early days proved very disappointing until it was realized that a club of this sort would meet with the utmost suspicion on the part of old lags everywhere.

'Don't want any b—— do-gooders getting at me!'

'What do they want with us? Some stuck-up people who think they're going to get their names in the paper for doing good, I should think!'

'Who are they anyway? Another of the same old thing —all right while you do what they tell you, and then— GET OUT!'

These and other remarks were heard on the 'grape-vine' and old friends relayed them rather apologetically as an excuse.

It was an interesting and revealing winter. On the financial side, with the support of the proceeds of the small café, the rent of the resident's flat let to a helper, and the small nightly takings, a profit of two shillings and elevenpence had been made at the end of the eight-month experimental period! The important thing was that no less than forty men used the club during that time, some were helped, many had jobs found for them, and although some only came a few times, others became regular members and seemed to enjoy having a place of their own. All this was done at no expense to the community.

The promoters of OLA were not selective. Anyone who had been in prison for any period over three months was welcome. This three months' rule avoided the club being used by that section of the prison population who continue to go in and out of prison on short sentences for drunkenness and are more of a medical problem than one connected with crime.

Men came who wanted lodgings, new arrivals from prison were often short of food. The machinery is there by which people just out of prison can get National Assistance, but as has already been seen from George's experience, few can plan it out carefully enough to last, with the result that many go hungry towards the end of the first week. Even if men have work, there is often the week-in-hand pay lag which makes life difficult.

Through the café it was possible to meet this demand, and meal tickets were sometimes given out to be repaid later when the man was earning. Some paid their dues, others did not, but at least they could not feel they were being offered charity.

Soon requests came along for special prisoners to be

met and helped on release. These were from welfare officers and after-care organizations in other cities, and even from the members of the prison administration. In such cases the help of those who had already been to the club was brought in, and every request was honoured. A few men were visited before release, and they were met on arrival and looked after for the first few days. Helpers went with them through the delays of National Assistance, to the Labour Exchange, and at last some of the difficulties and problems which George met became known through personal experience to the staff.

The man who, like George, had left prison without his breakfast, was met, the one who was too nervous to eat, yet needing his meal; such men were brought back to the club to sit in front of a warm·fire with a hot cup of tea until they could relax a little. Sometimes phone calls were made arranging appointments with particular officers of the N.A.B. or with an employer for an interview for a job.

The staff never got jobs for the men—they did that themselves. All that could be done was to get introductions. It was the rule that if a helper made an approach on behalf of a prisoner, the employer must be told of this fact, so that the permission of the member was always asked, otherwise he looked for his own employment. It has been found most wise for some responsible member of a firm to know if a man has a prison record, both for his own and the firm's safety. Employers were always most helpful about this, and usually the fact was known only to one or two responsible people.

Lodgings were a great difficulty. The staff had a few good addresses and they did what they could. A great need exists for more places willing to take ex-prisoners and give them accommodation. Often the men got their own lodgings, and this too presented difficulties. Very often the man had not said anything about his past, he just got his lodging in the ordinary way, and then found that the landlady had become suspicious.

Few people know how difficult it is for a man without possessions to get a room.

Some old lags have clothes that friends have kept for them during their time inside, but others have only the clothes they had when they were arrested. Long term men are fitted out with a minimum outfit by the prison, also the Statutory Organization have helped in providing tools and overalls in certain cases. All this takes time and at first a man may get a lodging and pay his week's rent, but he may only have the suit he stands up in and the small hold-all the prison provided.

After a week the landlady becomes suspicious and asks him when his other things are coming.

A man without possessions and only the clothes he is wearing is a doubtful character. The plan therefore was to collect men's clothing from friends, and keep a supply of them for needy people. Cases were also a necessity. Ex-prisoners feel terribly conspicuous to have only a prison bag, especially if it is one that anyone who knows the prison issue can recognize. It makes him feel a marked man, even though most people would not know. The staff therefore gladly accepted some old and rather battered cases which have proved to be a great help.

Karl was the first man in need of clothes. He had found a nice room and a very kind landlady, and it seemed everything was settled. After a few days, however, she began asking about his other things and when his luggage would be arriving. Afraid to say he hadn't got any he did what many an ex-prisoner would do in similar circumstances, and lied about it.

At last he brought the problem to OLA and a quick whip round produced a variety of articles from various sources. The staff had not been prepared for this, but all was well. Karl had his start and the rest was up to him.

If men get their own lodgings it is not necessary for them to tell anyone that they have been in prison. They just answer advertisements in the ordinary way, and this has proved to give them the best chance. If help can be provided by supplying extra necessary clothes it makes a man feel that he is like everyone else. In no case where such help was given to a man has he ever let the landlady down when he has been a member of OLA, but it has been found valuable to help in certain circumstances as there are often other lodgers in the same house and a prisoner who feels conspicuous rarely settles down to his new life.

Letters can be another difficulty. If a man gets lodgings he does not feel quite respectable unless he receives something through the post.

As time went on, family problems came along and even if help could not always be given at least staff could always provide a sympathetic ear, and occasionally a member would bring his wife or friend to the club and they were always welcomed.

So far men only have been mentioned in connection with the experiment of OLA. This is because in the particular area where the experiment took place there were no women's prisons anywhere near. Had any women come along they would have been equally welcome.

It was always felt that if a man decided to marry, and he was an ex-prisoner, it was only safe and right that he should inform his prospective wife of this fact before things became too serious.

As a rule men make many friendships amongst people who know nothing of their past, and this is right because they want to forget it; but where marriage is contemplated the position is entirely different. Sooner or later the truth is sure to come out, and nothing could be more disastrous if it is discovered and the wife then knows that her husband has deceived her.

Walter's was a case in point, and a rather interesting little story could be told about his engagement.

OLA knew him well, he was a member of the original club, before it changed over entirely to after-care. His record was of two fairly short sentences and he was free and working in the neighbourhood doing quite satisfactorily.

One evening he came to bring a very attractive young lady to the club and introduced her as the one he was going to marry. José was his girl and he was delighted with her.

Later he was asked if he had told her about his prison record, and that he should before things went any further.

'O, I couldn't,' he said. 'She'd turn me down, I know, I daren't.'

'Walter,' said the club leader, 'if you don't tell her, sooner or later someone will turn up who recognizes you and then the truth will be out. Far better to tell her now and then it won't matter. If you don't you'll always be afraid.'

'Well—perhaps after we're married . . .'

'No, Walter. That's not fair, and besides you'll never know where you stand if you don't tell her. If she truly loves you she won't turn you down, but if she doesn't then you'd far better know now.'

'Well—,' he hesitated. 'Perhaps I will, but not yet, please don't try and make me. I can't do it yet.'

It was left there, but the leader was worried and in a few days Walter came back.

'I've decided she ought to know,' he said. 'I thought it would be a good idea if you told her. She'll take it better from you.'

'Oh no, Walter! You can't get out of it that way,' said

the leader. 'I'm definitely not going to tell her. It's your job, now go and get on with it.'

Walter drooped visibly, and left the office like a small dog with its tail between its legs.

To the leader's great astonishment he was back inside half an hour, on top of the world. He burst into the office.

'I've done it!' he cried. 'And it's all right! She loves me, so it's all right!'

The leader was very surprised and asked Walter how he had managed it so well when he had been so frightened.

'It was like this,' he explained. 'Me and José went for a walk round the outside of the prison—you know, round by the wall. Well, when we were there, I said "José, do you see that wall?" and she said "Yes, Walter." "Well, José," I said, "I was once behind one of them walls-do-you-love-me?" and she said "Yes, Walter," so it's all right!!'

Prisoners often ask about owning up to past prison sentences. Men will frequently give their own experiences. 'Last time I was out I decided to be quite open about it,' said one man. 'Every place I went I said "I think you ought to know I've been in prison". The results were not encouraging. Some openly refused to employ me and others refused in a different way. "My dear chap, very good of you to tell me. I quite understand, but they're not all like me here. I would willingly give you a chance—glad to have you—but you know what it is—other people——" and sometimes "Here's five shillings, sorry we can't help".'

There are those who delight in making mischief, trying to get 'in' with the boss by telling tales.

'Mr Jones, can I see you privately for a few minutes?'

'Yes, Mr Skimper, what is it?'

'Well, sir, I've heard the men talking—it's about that new man you took on last week—Bloggs. It seems he's been in prison—just come out in fact—I thought you

H

ought to know—he may be all right—of course, I wouldn't mind—but—'

This places the boss in a difficulty. He remembers Bloggs, seemed a decent sort of chap, but hang it all, he didn't say where he'd been—some talk about having worked in the North—what was it? Perhaps after all it would be better not to keep him—might upset the others.'

So Blogg is out again and looking for work.

If Mr Jones had been asked if he would take a man out of prison and give him a chance, he would interview Bloggs rather differently. Knowing something of him from the probation officer, or social worker, Jones deliberately agrees to give Bloggs an opportunity. Not wanting to spoil Bloggs' chance Mr Jones limits the knowledge of his past to a few chosen people and the rest are not told. Again Skimper comes along with his whispered insinuations.

'Of course, sir—it may be a tale, but I thought you ought to know—.' This time Jones is ready for him, and Skimper has given himself away.

'Not a very nice sort of chap, that Skimper,' thinks Mr Jones. 'Always ready to push somebody down. After all, Bloggs was honest, he didn't tell me any lies.'

There are too many Skimpers about.

A few years ago a young man came to the original club who had served two six-month sentences for stealing. His home circumstances were such that he was no longer welcome in his parents' place and accommodation had to be found. One of the members at that time owned a long boat kept at local moorings and he offered most generously to take John to live with him on the boat. All went well for two months when one night the club member found a seedy looking individual lurking in the shadows near the moorings.

'Can I speak to you, Sir?' he said, shuffling up to him.

'What is it?'

'It's like this, Sir,' whined the seedy one. 'Down at the "Dove and Horse" people are beginning to talk—it's about that chap John.'

'Well, what about him?'

'You see, Sir, there's decent folk goes to that pub, and they don't like it having to drink with a felon.'

Resisting the temptation to push the seedy one into the canal, which he richly deserved, our member told him very plainly to mind his own business and clear off.

'But Sir,' he whined, 'It's more than that. Mr Johnson of the "Dove and Horse" owns the moorings and he says to tell you that either John is off the boat by the end of the week, or he won't renew your lease.'

So that was it. There was nothing to be done, it was a subtle form of blackmail, but moorings are not easily come by and the member brought the problem to the leader. Fortunately another place was found for John, and the situation was saved, but it is very easy to see what might have happened if John had been without friends. Almost inevitably he would have been forced back into crime, not by his own fault entirely, but pushed there by the people who might have helped him.

This again shows the great need for a place where someone is always available, someone who really cares. No one person can possibly do this. Obviously there is a need for a paid warden in charge, but there is also a place for volunteers who would be willing to do regular duties on a rota system. These other people, working under the guidance of the warden, would also get to know the prisoners, and make friends with them.

Voluntary helpers have often taken a special interest in one or other of the men and invited them to their homes. This has been an enormous help. Perhaps it has not always been realized what it is like for a man who has been in prison for many years to go into a private house and see a real coal fire burning on the hearth, to see a family with children and animals, and to feel welcome in a small close circle, perhaps even to drink a cup of tea out of a china cup by a fire.

The staff of OLA found that invitations to people's homes were long remembered by members. Months after an old lag had been invited to the home of a member of the staff for tea he wrote saying that the thing that had made so much difference to him in his early days at the club had been this acceptance as an ordinary guest. His letter said 'I often think about the time I was invited to tea and we sat round the fire eating toasted tea-cakes. The thing I liked so much was that the silver tea pot was used, just as if I were a friend of the family. I often think about it.'

People who have been fortunate do not know what such invitations mean to someone who has been in an institution for many years. No matter how comfortable such a place is made, nor how many extras are provided to help overcome bleakness, nothing can take the place of a real home.

Archie was a man who failed to keep out of prison, and was sentenced again. He wrote to the leader when he was back inside saying 'Do you know what I think about at nights in this place? It was that week-end I stayed in your home. I can picture it all now and it makes me remember that I must do better next time.'

The critic may say 'All very well. Anyone can talk like that, but it didn't stop him from getting into trouble again, did it?' That is true, but some men are already too much involved when they come out, too suspicious, too weak to make good, but if someone believes in them and is ready to try again, even then it is not too late, and there are men who have succeeded the second time who failed after the first freedom.

Occasionally there would be a night when no members turned up at OLA. Often there were only a few there, but always the men knew that some of the staff would be on duty, and that if they came someone would make them welcome. This constant provision of help is important. Those who know prisoners will realize how often in the first few months after release difficulties arise that are too big for the man to manage on his own. Cyril was an older man for whom the leader got work. He only came to the club three or four times altogether and then disappeared. It did not seem that he had really appreciated it at all. Some time later a letter was shown to the staff at OLA by the Governor of one of the prisons where Cyril had served a long sentence. It said 'I never went back to see those people at the club, but I often thought about them. It was good to know that there was always a place where you could go and be sure of finding friends.' Cyril had appreciated it after all.

The OLA experiment is only beginning. The first eight months proved the need for such work and it was decided to go on.

The story of George coming out of prison and the disastrous way in which he met his first few hours of freedom is proof that something different must be done to cater for such men. OLA is only one small effort, but it has already helped nearly eighty men since it began. Perhaps the time will come when other cities will run similar places. The initial cost of setting up a centre would not be very high if premises could be acquired at a sympathetic rent from the local authority. The experience of this first one has shown that gifts of good, but not too worn, second hand furniture are often forthcoming and apart from the café itself a great deal can be done at little cost compared with the purchase and furnishing of many buildings that have been set up all

over the country to tackle the problems of accommodation for ex-prisoners. The great advantage of OLA has
been that the running costs are covered by the café
business, and where the area is a good one for trade the
café might even provide an income for a resident leader.
One of the great disadvantages of most social work is not
the initial cost, for this can usually be raised by efforts
and gifts, but the continuing cost when the first enthusiasm
has gone is always hard to find.

Need does exist for accommodation for the ex-prisoner,
but a far greater need is for suitable places where he can
spend some of his leisure time. OLA is able to cater for
far larger numbers than any hostel can accommodate, and
a few such clubs in different parts of the country would
do much towards keeping men like George out of further
trouble. He failed because he did not have the right help
at the right time, and because nobody was really interested. His difficulties were those of many who come out
after years in prison.

He was lonely, frightened, over anxious to be indepen-
dent, hated to receive charity, especially as he really
needed help. He was unsure of himself, felt that people
were looking at him and recognizing him for what he was.
He needed a job and a place to sleep, but because he'd
been awkward he had not heard how he could get these
two essential things. Even if he had been told he would
still have been worried by the increased traffic, the need
to find his way about, and the embarrassment of having
to explain to so many people where he had been and
what he wanted. Ready to take offence at the first sign
of patronage, very suspicious of everybody and not at all
sure whether he really wanted to go straight, George was
like so many who have left prison in the same way.

The next chapter is a look into a possible future. A
centre has been imagined, somewhere in a city, catering

for the needs of ex-prisoners. A leader has been appointed, assisted by voluntary helpers, all people of understanding and good sense who are not easily taken in by plausible stories, yet knowing what to expect from a new man.

George is back in prison, of course. He was not likely to last long in freedom, but he has got to come out again. This time he is directed to the new centre and by tracing his story it will be seen how such a man could be helped.

The centre described does not exist at present, with its full time leader and experienced voluntary staff. On the other hand, George's reactions and the problems he faces are real, and his interesting response to the help provided has been pieced together from many incidents, by the staff of O L A from their own experience.

7

IT COULD BE DIFFERENT

George has been back for another stretch. Three months of freedom, and the police caught up with him. It had been a good time while it lasted, or so George kept telling himself. He had said so a great many times to the others —of course a fellow has to make a bit of a story out of it—never do to be strictly truthful, and anyhow, parts of it had been fun.

He'd had money—quite a lot of it. How quickly it went, though! One night, he remembered, they'd been out on a spree, and they ran out of cash. George had run round to the hotel where he had been staying and filled his pockets with handfuls of silver and small change from a case he kept under his bed—handfuls of it! God knew how much. That had been a good night; Mug-face and he had cleared all the takings from the dance hall before they made off—never counted it—just oodles and oodles of money, lovely money dripping through his fingers. Poppy had been a pretty little thing, too, and they'd had a good time. George had meant to keep up with Poppy— until the next day. Funny how girls could look so different in the morning, he thought.

It had been a good life, and of course he'd told the others it was worth it even if you did go *'up the steps'* at the end. He kept saying it was worth it, but was it really?

The best part of five years had gone by since then, and soon George would be outside again. Mug-face had gone down for longer, he'd had another charge, so he was a bit better off than that.

'Oh well!' thought George, as he lay thinking about his coming freedom. 'Tomorrow it'll be the same old tale again—same charity—same dreary day.'

'I'm getting too old for this,' he muttered. 'Suppose I'll have to give it up some time, but what could I do? Can't see myself going to work at 8.30 every morning and back at 5—to what anyway? Different for chaps with families —they've got something to go back to. Funny that new idea of the Governor's—this new place you have to go to for filling in forms and seeing about a job. It seems they've got you properly this time—not like the old days—got to be under compulsory supervision for a year now.'

George remembered supervision when he was a boy. 'Kid stuff, that's what it was—decent chap, though, that probation officer, but of course you only saw him once a week. Pity though things might have been different if I'd listened to him. Can't be any good now—not after all these years.'

George couldn't sleep. He kept thinking over the new kind of release. Mr Henry, that was the chap's name, who'd been to see him about it. You couldn't say you wouldn't see anyone now—not like the old days. This man had been to see him from the new centre, and said they'd be looking out for him on Wednesday. At least the man hadn't given him a lot of pious talk—seemed quite friendly, too, but then, they always were, these do-gooders, when they first saw you! Things would be different tomorrow. He'd have to go to the centre, but after that—well—after that he'd be on his own.

He remembered he'd nearly told Mr Henry his brother was going to meet him. He almost wished he had now. 'Why didn't I?' he wondered. 'Curiosity, I suppose.

Might as well see if they have anything to offer, and there's not much a man can do until evening.'

Tossing and turning, George felt the old fears coming over him. 'Wonder if I've lost the knack,' he thought. 'What happens to a chap when he's too old and slow? Got to live somehow—or come back here.'

'Funny,' he thought. 'It was wet last time I got out—doesn't it ever stop raining? Suppose I'll be wet through again by the time I get to that centre, and there I'll sit till I've caught cold waiting for some chap to fill in a form. It'll be like doing another day inside—why can't they just let you go?'

Morning came at last, and, shivering, George got himself dressed. 'It's lonely,' he thought. 'No-one to talk to—it's that dreadful hour before any place is open—people all pushing past you—people, people, all going places—all belonging somewhere.'

'Smith will be on the gate this morning—better than last time,' he told himself as he stood waiting to be unlocked. 'Bit different from old Shorty last time—coo! I nearly knocked his nose in—all that talk about not liking my face!'

There was a surprise waiting for George before he left the prison that day. Mr Henry was in the gate with the officer Smith.

'Good morning, George,' he said, shaking hands, 'if you call it a good morning with all this rain. I've got my car outside and we'll go along to the centre in that. No sense in getting wet before you start, is there?'

Speechless for once, and full of suspicion, George, with Mr Henry, stepped out of the gate, and ten minutes later the car drew up at a place that looked like an office on the outside.

'Don't take any notice of the look of the place,' said Mr Henry, 'We only moved in here last week—it's a lot better in than out.'

Wondering greatly, George followed Mr Henry into a passage from which a door opened into a small room, where a bright fire was burning and some old but comfortable chairs were drawn up to it.

'Sit down and make yourself at home,' said his guide, 'and help yourself to a cigarette—they're in that box on the table.'

George sat down gingerly, waiting for the whole thing to disappear, but he carefully took a *tailor-made* cigarette out of the box and lit it furtively.

Mr Henry had gone out for a few minutes, giving George time to look round, but he was soon back with some papers, followed by a lady with two cups of tea and a plate of biscuits.

George was dumbfounded. He'd never seen anything like this before—had they made some mistake? Had they thought he was someone else? Anyway, the tea was very welcome and the warmth of it seemed to penetrate his frozen hands and feet.

'I—I never come out like this before, Sir!' he found himself saying, and then shut up quickly. It didn't do to show these people how you really felt, they might take advantage of it.

'We'll have our tea first, and then get down to business,' said Mr Henry, and before long George found himself saying quite a lot more than he had meant to say. It was true he'd thought about a job 'but you see,' he added, 'I've never done anything for the last 15 years—only burglary,' he added, and waited for the patronising look he expected to see after such a naïve remark. The look was not there. Instead Mr Henry got out some papers and began to ask him a few simple questions. These answered, they discussed work, and the type of job George felt he could do.

'You say you once worked for a builder; you know,

I think that might be a bit difficult just now—we've got the bad weather coming and work may not be very regular. Have you ever thought of a factory job?'

George hadn't, but he thought he might try one— 'Only look here, Mr Henry, I've heard about that sort of thing before. They don't pay you till you've worked there two weeks, and they don't want you if you haven't got an address.'

'Don't worry about that, George, we shall look after it —the job's the first thing.'

A telephone call to the Labour Exchange produced the information that a local hosiery factory needed a man in the stores and packing department, and would be prepared to take an ex-prisoner recommended by the centre. George could go down at 2.30 that day to the Labour Exchange to get his card and take it along to the firm for an interview.

'Now that's settled, and we'll look at the accommodation list,' said Mr Henry. 'Let me see—you said you wanted a room where you could look after yourself, when I came to see you. It may be a bit difficult, you know—having to cook for yourself. You wouldn't rather try for a place with full board?'

George clutched desperately at his new independence. 'I'd rather be on my own,' he said quickly.

'Very well then, I can understand how you feel, and as you'll be working near Mill Lane I've looked out two addresses where you may find a vacancy. They're not on the phone, but I don't think we'll be too late. I thought we'd go along and see if one of them will do—that is unless you'd rather go and make your own arrangements?'

'I must be dreaming,' thought George, 'This isn't true —there's a catch coming in a minute—job found and accommodation too—why it isn't ten o'clock yet.' He heard himself saying 'Thank you, Sir, I'd be glad to get fixed up,' and thought 'I'll ruddy well get out if I don't like it, but it'll be nice to have somewhere to go tonight.'

As if he read his thoughts, Mr Henry went on 'Of course, you don't have to stay there if you don't like it, but it's a bit strange at first when you come out, and it will give you somewhere to live until you can make your own arrangements. Mrs Connolly at 27 has had men through us before. You'll find the room is clean and quite comfortable, if you take that one, and she won't ask too many questions.'

A telephone call to the National Assistance Board followed, and another form had to be filled in which would be taken along to the office if the job were secured.

'You see, we don't get the job for you, George. You have to get that yourself. We just make the appointment. Now if you're ready we'll go out and find those lodgings. If Mrs Connolly has got a room vacant and you like it you can leave your holdall there and go back with the money after you've collected something from the National Assistance.'

Back in the car, feeling more dazed than ever, George pinched himself to see if he were really there. They were not long finding the address and as the car drew up Mr Henry said 'I think you'd like to go in alone, wouldn't you? I'll wait in the car and see how you get on. If the room's gone we'll try the other address.'

George panicked. He wanted to go in alone, wanted to be free to sort things out, but he couldn't. 'I'd rather you came in too, Sir' he found himself saying.

The room was all right and the holdall was left there with the promise that George would pay when he got his money. Back at the centre once more, Mr Henry stopped the car. 'Now I've got one or two things to do and I expect you'd like to be on your own for a bit. It's only eleven o'clock, and I suggest you have a walk round

and then come back here about 1 p.m. I can fix you up
with a meal, and then someone will run you down to the
NAB and the Labour Exchange.'

Alone at last, George found himself walking away from
the centre, past some shops, watching people—free
people—and wondering if they could tell where he'd
come from.

'I'm free now,' he said to himself, 'I needn't go back.
I can just clear off—I've got my five shillings and I don't
need any b-do-gooder—I'm FREE!' It was a lovely feeling.
Turning into a milk bar he ordered coffee and bought
some fags. He found he was quite glad to sit at a table in
a corner and just smoke quietly while he tried to think
things out.

He needn't go back—he could clear out now—but if
he did where would he go? That was a bit of luck last
time, meeting Mug-face, but he wouldn't be there—he
was still inside—standing there with his tray collecting his
lunch—and won't be out for months yet. 'I'm lucky, aren't
I?' he mused, 'If ever I want to try and go straight this is
the time if all they've said is true about the job. I think
I'll go back to the centre anyway. I'll get some lunch and
I might as well eat. The chap's been decent so far—none
of that talking down to a fellow—might as well get all I
can before there are any snags.'

Lunch was provided in a small café next door to the
centre, which Mr Henry explained belonged to it. 'Of
course, anybody can use the café, but it gives us a chance
to provide a few meals for chaps like you. Mrs Davies
will write down what you spend and let me know. When
you're settled in your own job you can pay it back. I'm
meeting a train this afternoon, because we're expecting
two more men, but one of my colleagues will be at the
centre and we've arranged for him to see you through the
National Assistance and take you to the factory. I shall

be back here this evening, so if you care to look in later you can tell me how you've got on.

George found himself a bit embarrassed when he was handed the menu. How funny that it was so difficult to choose and decide even about a simple thing like food, when you've never had to choose anything for years. He must have hesitated a long time because the waitress said 'There's a very good steak and kidney today if you like that.' George did, but he wasn't going to be told what to have, so he said he thought he'd have some fish, and then wished he hadn't. However, the fish was quite good and plenty of it. 'What happens next?' he thought. 'Mr Henry said they'd keep an account but he's not here now, and what if they ask me for the money?' In a feeling of sudden panic George felt in his pocket—trying to see how much of the five shillings was left, without actually taking the money out, but the waitress must have been watching, because she brought him a cup of tea and said 'It's on your account and you can settle with them later on at the centre.'

Feeling bewildered, but better for a good hot meal, George went back to the other building where he was met by a new man who had the forms that had been filled in earlier. This man introduced himself as Mr Simpson and explained that different helpers came along on a rota system so that there was always someone on hand to help as new men arrived.

'I see your appointment at the Labour Exchange is at 2.30 p.m. so we'll take the forms and go down there first, and after that we'll collect the money from the National Assistance.'

In the car going down George remembered the hours of miserable waiting about that lay before him. He recalled the room full of rows of wooden benches and the queues of people. 'Don't suppose it will be any different—it won't have changed much since the last time,' he said to himself, 'But at least I've had a meal and I'm not wet through.'

At the Labour Exchange he found he was expected, and Mr Simpson didn't go in by the ordinary door, but through to a small office in another part of the building where an officer checked through the papers already filled in and after a few more questions the card about the job was handed out. 'You ask for Mr Jones, who knows you are coming. He knows that you have just come out of prison, but if they decide to employ you there is no need to worry. It won't be known in the factory. Of course I must make it clear to you that if you want to change your job or if it doesn't suit you, then you will have to go through all the ordinary channels just as any other man. This special arrangement today only applies to men just out from prison, so that they can get a fresh start. You'll find Smiths a good firm to work for. If you play fair with them, they'll play fair with you.'

Driving to the factory George was horribly nervous. Beads of sweat stood out on his forehead. 'Oh hell!' he thought, remembering what he'd heard from other men inside. 'What a fool I shall look if anyone sees me going in.' Feeling cornered and longing to run away—yet wanting to get the job and make a start, George knew he'd never have gone there at all if he'd had to do it alone. Sensing his feelings, Mr Simpson drove slowly, talking easily as they went along.

'It's a bit of an ordeal, all this, isn't it? You must be wondering what it's all about, and tired after meeting so many different people today. Most men are, but it has to be done, and you'll feel all right about it when things are settled.'

Mr Jones of Smith's seemed to know all about him when at last George got to his office. On the defensive, as usual, George had his story all ready, he'd planned what he would say. 'Yes, he'd just come out, so what? What had he done? Well, he'd been in a bit of financial difficulty some years ago now—wife had left him—taken the kids and he was off his balance—don't know why—couldn't remember taking that money—wouldn't have done it if he hadn't been upset at the time over the wife,' etc., etc. 'They always fell for a hard luck story—better say something so that it sounded good—wonder what the old so and so would say if he knew the truth!'

No questions were asked about his past. Mr Jones told him about the job he would be required to do, and said the men wouldn't be told anything about the prison record. If he did his work well and kept good time, he'd have nothing to worry about. 'If you are in any difficulty you can ask to see me and we'll sort it out,' he said, as he got up to show the interview was over. 'We'll see you on Monday next at 8.30, then, Brown.'

'Only one more call, George,' said Mr Simpson, and then you'll be able to go to your room and do as you like. I'm sure you'll be relieved when all the necessary arrangements are made and you can begin to feel settled.'

'Settled!' thought George, 'I bet I'll feel settled all right when I've sat in that "B" National Assistance waiting room for a few hours. It's been a funny sort of day so far, but now we really are going to begin. Guess I'll take the money and clear off—pity I left that holdall at the digs—still it's prison stuff and I'll have to scrap it—hope they give me a week's money, though.'

The streets were full of traffic, and secretly George was thankful he was in the car. 'Can't seem to get the hang of it yet,' he thought. 'Seems to be so noisy and far more cars and buses than I remember last time.'

'Nearly there now,' said Mr Simpson, driving down a narrow side street between two large buildings.

I

'It doesn't look like the old place,' said George, 'Guess these skyscrapers weren't here when I was out last time.'

'They haven't been here long. They only moved last August. We'll park just here because we're not going in the public entrance today. There's a Miss Wright who always sees my new men from the centre. Have you got the card from Mrs Connolly's about your room, because they'll want to see that to get confirmation of the booking?'

Papers were again handed in and Miss Wright examined them, applied a stamp with the date, and 'phoned through some code number to another department.

'We don't expect you to queue up in the public hall when you first come here in your circumstances, Mr Brown,' she said. 'We make different arrangements for the first fortnight because we know you don't get your wages until you have worked a week in hand. I see you will be paying £2 for the room, and you will need another fifty shillings for food. That will make a total of £4 10s for each of the next two weeks until you get your first pay. You will have £3 10s now so that the room rent is paid for, and the rest of the fortnight's allowance will be paid to you at the centre on the two coming Mondays. You will give the card to Mr Henry after the week-end, and he will see that you are all right.'

'Well, strike me pink!' muttered George, 'They've sure given a face lift to the National Assistance since last time! It certainly makes it a bit easier coming out than it used to be'—but to himself he thought 'I wonder when I'll begin to find the snags? It won't be long now, I expect. They're sure to be up to something.'

Mr Simpson left him at the digs—but first he said 'I'm sure you'll be glad to be on your own for a bit. I'll just drive you back to Mrs Connolly's so you can pay for your room, and then I must get back to the centre. You'll find us around later in the evening if you feel like a bit of company. We never close until 10.30 but if you'd rather be on your own we shall understand.'

George was really tired. He didn't go out again that night except to the café at the corner opposite his room where he had a cup of tea and a sandwich. He had meant to go to the pub that evening to see if any of the chaps were there, but that could wait.

The next morning George stayed in bed late. It was good to feel he hadn't got to get up—besides, so much had happened he needed time to think about it all. He'd got a job to go to on Monday, he'd got a room of his own and money in his pocket. Today he could do as he liked, walk around, go to the pictures, sit in the local—yes, and if he liked he could call at the centre where he'd see someone he knew. It might be a good idea too—after all, they'd been pretty decent.

That day George began to find his way around, but the traffic was a problem, and lunch time found him in the centre café. The waitress recognized him and nothing was said about the free meal he'd had the day before. This time he paid for his meal like the rest. During lunch Mr Henry came in and paused to speak to him.

'Call in tonight at the centre, if you like,' he said. 'You'll find several men like yourself there, and some other people. There's a T.V. and you can get refreshments. By the way, do you play chess?' George did. He'd learned in prison. He wasn't brilliant, but he could hold his own in a game.

'I can always look in for an hour and see what it's like, and then go to the pub,' he thought, but when he finally walked in after he'd seen the whole programme at the nearby cinema it was already nine o'clock. Four men were there, one of whom he'd seen before inside, and several other poeple who turned out to be 'friends' of the centre.

Taffy recognized him, but waited to see what George would do. Taffy had only done two short sentences, George might not want to speak, but he did. It was good to see someone he knew. Taffy and he sat in a corner chatting about familiar places.

'What do you make of this centre, Taff?' asked George. 'Been coming here long?'

'They only moved into these rooms last week, but they've had a centre for a year now. It's all right, too. I got a bit of a shock myself when I came here first, but they really do help you. I don't come in every night—two or three times a week, I should think—you can bring a friend along and it's useful when you've got an hour to spare.'

Just then a man came and joined them, talking easily, and handing round cigarettes.

'My name's Forsyth,' he said, 'I always come in on Wednesdays. I expect this seems a bit strange to you, being new to us, but you see we've about twenty "friends" of the centre, and we arrange to be here when we can. Mr Henry is in charge and lives here, but the rest of us are voluntary helpers so you'll see us quite often if you come in.'

Conversation was easy with Mr Forsyth. He didn't ask a lot of questions, but he seemed keen on sport and George picked up some useful information about local football teams. He forgot he'd meant to go to the pub, the time passed quickly and before he realized it he saw that it was after ten.

'I wonder if you'd care to come round to my house if you're not doing anything on Saturday,' said Mr Forsyth as they were leaving. 'The week-ends usually drag a bit when you're new to a place.'

'I—I'd like that' said George hesitatingly. 'Wonder if he knows who I am?' he thought.

'Well that's fine. I'll pick you up here at about 3 on Saturday afternoon and take you home for tea. My missus is a pretty good cook and the kids always like a visitor. So long then, I'll be seeing you.'

'Well, I don't know?' thought George as he walked back to Mrs Connolly's. 'Two days ago I was doing my bird, and here I am with a ruddy job, a place to live and some money for food, and an invitation to someone's home. Can you beat it?' Of course, there were another two days before that happened, and maybe he wouldn't be around—or maybe he would. It would be nice to be in a real home again, and see kids too. Must be years since George had been in a family—'It might be worth going once, anyway,' he decided.

Next day George decided to give the centre a miss. 'Wouldn't do to give them ideas,' he thought. He ate a good lunch in a café, saw another film, and went to the local as soon as he came out. This was more in his line, he thought, but he hadn't much money left. 'Oh well, what's money for if it isn't to spend and enjoy yourself?' he thought.

In the morning he was broke. His head ached and he decided to stay in his room. He'd got some tea and a bit of sugar—he'd wait until evening and then see—perhaps he could try his old luck—might pick something up. If he didn't get caught he'd try the job—give it a week and see what going straight would do. He would like to go to Forsyth's home on Saturday, he really would.

Thinking over plans and drinking his tea he was surprised when Mrs Connolly knocked at his door.

'There's Mr Henry called to see you, Mr Brown,' she said, smiling. 'He's here right now.'

'Well, George, I thought I'd just come along and see how you were getting on. It's a difficult week, isn't it? You'll feel more settled when you're working.'

'I'll get another cup if you'd like some tea,' said George, 'But I'm afraid I've forgotten to get any milk.'

Mr Henry was no fool. He guessed what had happened, and he came straight to the point.

'I rather think you may find it difficult to make out on the money this week, George,' he said. 'So I've got a plan. A good many chaps find it awkward at first, not used to having to lay out the money so that it will last. Now we've got a job at the new centre that we need some help with. Have you ever done any painting?'

Seeing George's expression, he continued: 'I thought so—well, it's like this. Could you give us a bit of help on decorating the premises this week-end? We can't afford to pay anyone to do it, but we can provide meals. I thought perhaps you might come back with me now—I've got some overalls that would fit you, and when we've had something to eat we'll get down to it.'

George went along. He ate, he worked, he stayed at the centre that evening for he'd nothing else to do, and he got to know some more of the helpers. On Saturday he was there when Mr Forsyth called for him, and he had his first real tea with a family for ten years. On leaving he got another invitation for the next week-end. Only one big difficulty now lay ahead—work! George hadn't worked in an outside job for so long that he knew he just couldn't make himself go. His legs wouldn't carry him.

Lying in bed on Sunday night he decided he'd have to go to the centre on Monday evening and collect his National Assistance money, then he'd blow. He could almost see himself telling Mr Henry—and then he knew he just couldn't lie to the man. He knew he couldn't go to the job but he'd just clear off—leave the place—he wouldn't take that money from Mr Henry because he'd been good to him. One day he'd maybe write and tell him how much he'd appreciated what Mr Henry had done for him, but you couldn't expect a man like that to understand why he couldn't go to work.

Next morning George got up early; better not let Mrs Connolly know he wasn't going to work—he'd have to go out—he'd have to leave his things—pity, but he'd manage somehow.

Outside the door Mr Simpson was waiting with his car.

'Good morning,' he called. 'I expect you feel a bit nervous about this new job—so I thought I'd come along and give you a lift. It's always bad starting the first day, but once that's over you'll be fine.'

So there it was. George went to work, found he could manage the job, and nobody asked questions or stared at him. He collected his money and spent the evening at the centre. The first crisis was over.

There are readers who will say that George was given too much help and that he was extremely ungrateful. I can only say that had the help not been available, George would be back inside by now, because the fears and doubts from which he suffered are common to many who come out after years in prison. Unless the help had been imaginative, it would not have succeeded, but Mr Henry and some of his staff could feel what was going on in George's mind, and they were ready to help him—not by offering charity, which would have made George feel inferior, but by doing some ordinary acts of friendship in an understanding way.

It would be easy to say that George started work and went back to the centre, and they all lived happily ever after. It would make after-care a lot easier if that were true. The fact is that although they had got George through his first crisis there were bound to be more to come. The problems and difficulties that beset those who have just come out are manifold, and it is the continuing after-care that really counts in the rehabilitation of ex-prisoners.

More will be said of George and the next phase of his story in the next chapter, but there may be a few people who can see in this brief description of the centre a possibility for the future development of after-care of a new type.

Something will have to be provided that is more suited to the needs of ex-prisoners than anything we have so far been able to achieve. The Governments of many countries as well as our own are concerned about the problem and many ideas are being discussed.

It is surely possible for a committee of people to plan something on the lines of Mr Henry's centre. We have made a start, but we have a long way to go. The plan will involve many people who are prepared to give not only money but time. These people must be able to face disappointment and disillusionment but must have courage and faith to go on. Centres like the one described could fill a great need in every big city, and the first days of freedom could be quite different if the right help could be available.

I have found many men and women over the years who were willing to give voluntary service to help handicapped people. It has always been possible to recruit volunteers if one or two will take a lead and start something. The difficulty is always to find the pioneers. Perhaps there may be amongst the readers of this book some who will like our experiment and develop it so that coming-out needs may be met.

Mr Henry's centre could help with other problems of release, and we will now follow George through some of these and see what happened to him, and the way in which he was helped.

8

NOT ONLY COMING OUT

It is obvious that the initial help suggested for men and women on release from prison is very important, and that steps should be taken to set up other centres where the first few days or weeks of change can be catered for in better conditions.

It is true that much more could be done to avoid the early return to crime which so frequently happens in cases where the first insuperable difficulties have literally driven men and women to return to their old known life. Men have often been heard to say 'For two pins I'd have jumped on a train those first few days and gone back to the place I used to "work" in. I couldn't see how I could settle down to the new type of life, and if it hadn't been . . .' etc. etc. They know that without the initial help they couldn't have got through.

After-care does not end with the first week. It is a continuing process over quite a long period, sometimes years, and the value of a centre is that help is always at hand when the various crises of ordinary every day life appear.

It is difficult to realize at first what these crises are, so once again a story relating to an actual old lag may be appropriate.

Johnnie was thirty years of age. His history was not unlike that of many inadequate people. He came from an artisan home where his father was a weak but respectable citizen. His mother—a positive virago—a militant member of a religious order, who continually criticized and carped and beat her young son so that he would always behave in a manner likely to be accepted as proper by the neighbours.

Johnnie learned to be cunning at an early age by deceiving his mother about money matters. Minor offences and later truancy from school brought Johnnie to the attention of the authorities and before long a period of probation was followed by a few years in an approved school. Weak and inadequate, he drifted on until he finally ended up in prison, rejected by his family for long intervals and occasionally restored to favour between sentences until the nagging references to past conduct drove him out once more to return to minor thefts and deceptions. Johnnie married, but his wife soon left him for another man, and finally he was committed to prison for five years, because more serious offences had been committed.

Efforts were made on his release to find suitable employment and lodgings but the burden of independence proved too much and during a fit of depression a shop window was deliberately broken by Johnnie in order to return to prison where he could be safe and warm through the winter months and not have to decide anything. Twice more this happened, until even Johnnie came to realize he'd have to make some effort unless he wished to spend the rest of his life inside.

At first he managed fairly well, and a day to day contact was made so that he could be sure of finding some friendly person through a club. None of the members knew his background, except the leader, and all seemed to be going well. He found a new girl friend, and Johnnie began to feel that life was really getting quite good for him.

One thing he had promised, and it was that if ever he

felt particularly tempted to go back to the old life he would come and tell the club leader first. This he had actually done on one or two occasions, and curious as it may seem this kind of thing frequently happens with old lags, almost as if they were trying, as a last resort, to get someone to help them and stop them from slipping back. So far the leader had always been available, but this was mostly by luck. It had not been realized at that time the need for several people to share this duty so that there would never be days when help was unobtainable.

Calamity came when Zoe—the new girl friend—suddenly left the city and disappeared. Johnnie panicked, and nearly went off at once feeling that the bottom had dropped out of his world, as indeed it had.

Frequently on such occasions even the most important promises are forgotten and a man thrown completely off balance will resort to violence or crime as though some sub-conscious part of his brain had taken control, but Johnnie did remember and came to the club to seek help. Unfortunately the leader was away from the city and was not available until the next day.

Johnnie just couldn't wait.

No one else in the club knew his history, nor of the promise he had made.

On the leader's return it was to learn that Johnnie had disappeared, nor was there any further news of him until a newspaper disclosed that Johnnie had committed another crime and was sentenced to ten years' preventive detention.

He is still serving that sentence. Such help as can be given in the circumstances has been provided, and friendly relations have been maintained by regular visits and letters.

It has ever since been clear that the need exists for

some such place as Mr Henry's centre where, in the absence of the leader or welfare officer in charge, someone else with knowledge of the members would always be on duty. The burden of providing this continuing after-care is a heavy one, as all probation officers know, but there are volunteers who can be brought in to take certain duties—perhaps weekly, just for a few hours—who can relieve and help by their own friendly knowledge of the members, and be ready to cope with situations like that of Johnnie.

Homeless and inadequate people need someone to whom they can turn in an emergency. They manage fairly easily when things go smoothly, but break down quickly under extra strain and frustration.

Quite a number of difficult situations can arise which are so closely related to the past life in prison that they are almost incomprehensible to ordinary people and there is a real need for after-care helpers who have an understanding of such situations.

Let us return to George, and see how some of these unusual stresses and strains will affect his rehabilitation.

He has been free now for three weeks. He knows a number of people at the centre, and has met several men there with whom he has done *time*. He has overcome his first natural suspicion of Mr Henry and his staff; although only just. He believes they really want to help him, and he's almost satisfied that they are doing it because they believe in him and not because they are hoping someone else will reward them for it. He'd like to believe they were genuine, but one part of him keeps being wary because the kind of help he has had so far is unknown in his world, and he sometimes wonders still when he will wake up and find it's all gone, and he's back to the old routine of previous years.

George often thinks about Flinty who will be out before

long. He knows that sooner or later he is bound to meet him, and after all Flinty helped him last time so he may reasonably expect George to pay him something. Flinty was a big man in the prison, a tobacco baron, and little men inside found him useful at first. Later they feared him greatly because they owed him money. George himself owed him £2 which to anyone outside may seem a paltry amount. Inside, however, it represents a lot where money values are quite different. It takes a man many months to collect such a sum. In the old lags' code such a debt must be paid some time. Men have only one way open to them of discharging the debt if they cannot pay—that is to try and escape from the prison. There is just a chance that they may get right away, although usually they are caught and brought back, but the fact that they are then punished and lose all their remission wipes out the debt, for the baron has then not lost face. His 'slaves' have been shown to fear him so much that they risked escaping rather than admitting the debt and their inability to pay. Some of the breaks from long-term prisons are well known as 'tobacco breaks', and may not always be understood by those who know nothing of the fears and values of the life inside. If a man leaves prison at the end of his sentence without paying the baron, he may go in fear for the rest of his life, for the baron on release will either seek him out himself or get some of his satellites to do it for him. Standards by which prisoners live are almost those of the jungle, but they are very real, as one man can testify whose face was cut from top to bottom with a razor because he had failed to pay a small sum of money owed to a baron, and the baron himself would have lost his own position as leader of the pack had he failed to seek retribution. The man knew why he had been injured and there was nothing he could do about it.

To return to George, the law of the jungle had been

his life for many years, and he knew the approaching fear of Flinty's release.

He knew he ought to have paid Flinty that money somehow, and he had met Jones in the pub one evening who had told him that Flinty had only one more month to do. Outside it is easy to see a solution to this, but George thinks as an old lag thinks, and his mind works quite differently.

Mr Henry had noticed that George seemed different, he was preoccupied and then for several days he hadn't been to the centre at all.

'Have you noticed that George Brown hasn't been in lately?' he asked one of the volunteer helpers.

'Oh he was in last Sunday night—I saw him talking to Mr Forsyth.'

'Yes, I saw him then also, and he seemed a bit off balance I thought.'

'Well, I expect he'll turn up again soon—perhaps he's found a new girl-friend. They always do sooner or later.'

'Well, keep a look out for him and if he does come in let me know. If he's away much longer I'll call round. He's only been out three weeks, so anything may have happened.'

However, they had not long to wait.

Walking by the 'Owl's Nest' one evening that week, George ran right into Sparky, a jovial sort of chap who'd shared a cell with him and Mug-face for many months. Over a drink, Sparky told the news of the old nick since they'd last been together, and many a good laugh they had thinking of the old days. All at once Sparky said 'Remember Flinty?' George stiffened. 'That B's a right rogue if ever there was one. Glad I don't owe him anything. What do you think? Young Ted on C wing's left without paying for his snout and Flinty hasn't half got it in for him—he says he'll find him if it takes him years, and I wouldn't like to say what Ted's face'll be like when he's finished with him. . . . Say—what's the matter with you? You look as if you'd had somebody walk over your grave! Here, come on George, have another drink. Never thought you'd go all sissy hearing about someone's face being slashed.'

But George couldn't agree. He tried to crack a feeble joke with Sparky, made some lame excuse about seeing a *bird*, and got up to go.

'Well, I'm damned,' said Sparky. 'You've sure got it bad, you have, and at your age too—bet she can't be all that good'—and, as George retreated, 'Poor old sod, you'd never have thought it!'

Outside George quickly slipped away into the darker streets, merging with the crowd, hands in pockets, head down, shoulders hunched, and he walked for a good hour trying to think what he'd better do. Flinty would find him, for sure, and if it wasn't Flinty it would be one of them— Flinty's shadows, always ready to go after someone for what he pays them.

'Yes,' he thought, 'I'd better *blow*—too easy to find me here, and Flinty never forgets. I'm for it, too, like poor Ted—wonder if Sparky knew and was trying to warn me? No—he'd have said—lucky thing I went in there—better keep clear though. First place Flinty'll try, that is.'

Tired but sleepless, George lay awake planning. He'd got about a week, he thought, and no more than that, before the danger began. He'd have to make off then, but on second thoughts he'd better go tomorrow—better be right out of the district. He felt cornered—trapped— just when he'd got a real start, and he quite liked his job, too.

'Knew there'd be some snags in it,' he thought, 'and here they are.'

Next day his work was poor, and the foreman noticed

and made some sarcastic remark about it. Angry and in no mood for criticism, George glowered at him. 'Who does the "B" think he is, anyway?' he thought.

Diverted from his main worry George did his obstructive best to get his own back for the slight, and when the whistle blew he'd nearly got himself the sack. Rebellious and desperate, tired from the lack of sleep and all the worry, George decided he'd *blow* that night—should he go to the centre first? 'No, if I did they may make me change my mind,' he said to himself, and he didn't want that—or did he?

At last he told himself it wouldn't work, anyway, because this time he'd got to go. 'Oh hell,' he thought. 'Why didn't I pay that money to Flinty? It's hopeless— you never get away from the old life, it always catches up on you.'

Thinking furiously George found himself walking by the centre café—almost as if by habit he turned in at the door, got inside—thought "They've been good to me and I'll miss them—perhaps. . . .'

'Hello, George,' said Mr Henry, coming in at that moment. 'We've missed you this week-end and I was coming round to look you up if you hadn't turned up tonight.'

George felt a wave of anger suddenly creeping over him. 'Why the hell couldn't they leave a chap alone—he was free, wasn't he? Interfering old so and so—why did he have to come in just then?'

Mr Henry knew his man—he'd met George before— and he saw that sudden fleeting look, so he said, smiling 'Well, perhaps that was going a bit too far. Naturally you've got your own life to live and your own new friends. Take no notice of what I said, it's only that we've got used to having you around and we've missed you. I was just going to have a coffee sent into my office. Hi! Mrs

Prentice—can you bring along another cup for George here?' and turning to George again he went on talking naturally, observing but apparently ignoring the tense expression on George's face.

Sitting by the fire in the chair he had first occupied three weeks ago, George relaxed a little, but he was unresponsive and quiet, knowing as he did that he wouldn't sit there again. Coffee and a cigarette failed to relieve all the tensions, and presently he blurted out 'I'm not staying at that job, Mr Henry. They're not playing fair with me—can't do anything right, I can't. Expect they've got it in for me because I'm an "ex".'

This was a good way to do it, he thought. 'Let Mr Henry think I'm unsettled at work, and then when I don't turn up he'll think that's it. Good idea of mine,' and his ever lively imagination took hold of the idea so that he soon embarked on a whole recital of incidents, some completely fictitious, to account for his mood.

Mr Henry got out his pipe and settled down to listen to George, smoking quietly and without interrupting. At last George became silent too, even his inventive genius had petered out. Annoyed again that Mr Henry was apparently taking it all so calmly he said rather truculently 'Well?'

'Well, George, from what I've seen of you this last three weeks I'd have thought you were an intelligent man, but what you've told me is neither intelligent nor sensible, and not like you at all, so I'm waiting.'

'What do you mean about knowing me? You don't know only one bit of me—none of you do,' bridled George.

'I know you came out three weeks ago, and you made up your mind you'd give it a chance and try and go straight. You've settled down a bit and you've got friends, but you know it isn't that easy. There are always difficul-

K

ties, like awkward foremen, and you were bound to meet some of those. I'm not surprised you're feeling edgy, most of us do when things have gone wrong, but that's just when friends come in handy. Now what you've been telling me makes it quite clear that something has gone wrong for you. Knowing you, even a little bit, George, I don't think it's your work entirely, because only last week I saw Mr Jones and he gave me a very satisfactory report. Wouldn't it be a good idea if you told me what started all this? Two heads are better than one.'

Sullenly George muttered 'I'm through! You've done your best for me, but you can't clear up this mess.'

'Perhaps not, but I shall know better when I've heard about it. I know it's something pretty serious, or you wouldn't be so worried.'

George took another cigarette out of the box on the table, and smoked it rapidly. Mr. Henry waited, puffing quietly at his pipe.

'I guess I shouldn't have lied to you. I shouldn't have come in here tonight because you can't help me. Nobody can. The fact is I shan't be around here much longer. I shall miss coming in, I'd like you to know I'm grateful for what you've done for me. Maybe if I'd known you before my last *bird* I'd have done better, but it's too late now.'

'Then it's something from the past catching you up?' said Mr Henry quietly. 'But tell me this, George, if this thing hadn't turned up, you'd have been happy to stay on here, wouldn't you?'

'Yes, I'm all right here. I'd like to stay, but I can't, that's it. I can't explain, but I've got to go.'

'Are you sure it won't catch up with you again, even if you do go, George? Every place you go it'll catch up on you sooner or later. Have you thought of any other way round the problem that wouldn't mean running away?'

'Who says I'm running away?' shouted George, starting to his feet. 'Now look here, Mr Henry, you're a good sort, and I don't want to be rude to you when you've helped me, but nobody's going to tell George Brown he's running away.'

Mr Henry said quite quietly 'Very well, George, if you mean to go you're free to do so, but I would like to tell you something first, if you can spare a few minutes more.'

George hesitated, his hand on the door knob, but he stayed where he was.

Without any outward sign of anxiety Mr Henry continued. 'We were expecting a new man last week who was to have come from Fentown prison. I'd visited him several times in the last two years, and he seemed to have everything in his favour for a good start. It is exactly two months ago that I last visited him and the very next day he escaped over the wall in the night. It was a carefully planned break out, and he knew when I was visiting him that he was going that way within hours. He didn't get far, and he was back inside within the week. I read about it in my paper, and when I went back to see him shortly after he'd lost all his remission and the job he was going to get but he was happy—as if a weight had gone off his mind. Micky, I'll call him, was sorry he'd let me down, but he had wiped his slate clean by running away.'

'He must have owed money to some bloke inside that he couldn't pay,' said George, turning round and re-seating himself at the fire.

'Yes, you're right, George, but do you think by any chance that if he came here as we'd planned he might have had to run away later on if the money hadn't been paid back?'

'He could have moved to a new district, couldn't he?' replied George, 'and he could have made a fresh start.'

'But one day they'd have caught up with him, one day

someone might have come along for that money. Micky would always have been afraid.'

'But what else could he have done, Mr Henry?' asked George, leaning forward. 'That Micky did the best thing for himself when he went over the wall. He'd only have got *choky* and lost his remission. I only wish I'd . . .'

'Yes, George?'

'Well, I suppose I may as well tell you seeing you know about it already. If I'd done what Micky did I wouldn't be in this mess. I didn't pay, and I didn't run, so now I'm for it.'

'How much, George?'

'It's only £2, and it doesn't sound much to you, I expect, but it was more than I could pay inside, and I thought I'd been clever, and got out and no one would find me.'

'And now?'

'Well, I saw one of the chaps down at the "Owl's Nest" and the baron will be coming out before the end of the month. The chap was warning me, I reckon, and I tell you, Mr Henry, I don't want my face slashed, one of these days, because I haven't paid the money."

"You haven't got £2 yet?"

"It's not that. I could get the money this Friday, but that wouldn't get it to Flinty.'

Mr Henry understood, he saw it all very clearly, knowing something of the prison code, and the immature way in which the old lag takes fright and doesn't allow himself to think reasonably about things. There was only one chance for George, and it wasn't too late, if the money could be sent to the prison to be kept for Flinty on his release. He spoke of this to George, saying that this could be done. 'You really think so? Flinty leaves in a week, so we haven't much time. He'd know it was from me, all right—we could say it was from George.'

So it was arranged. Mr Henry wrote the letter and the money was posted on Friday night after George got his pay packet. Mr Henry rang the prison himself to make sure the man was still there, and they were in time.

The first big crisis had been averted. George was able to remain at his job, and in time he settled down again, doing his work well enough to satisfy the foreman. He didn't thank Mr Henry—at least not then—and the matter was not referred to again. This may seem to some to be ungrateful but those who work with prisoners don't look for gratitude. One day, later on if George makes it, he will do something for Mr Henry and it will be understood that he is paying back the debt he owes him. Nothing will be said. That is the code.

Not all men are involved like George, but some are, and have thrown away their chances of a steady job and a new beginning through the lack of a trusted friend to advise and help.

Paul, another man using the centre, had a crisis of a different sort, but one well known to all who do after-care.

He was a man who had served four short sentences for shop-lifting. Well known in his own district, Paul would go straight after release for about two or three weeks, and then, having got tired of managing on his small regular wage, would begin to hang about Department Stores—particularly in the radio department. Transistor sets were his line, and sooner or later certain of them would disappear from the store and be sold to anyone who would pay Paul's modest price. He was not very intelligent because he failed to appreciate that the police were not fools and before long he would find himself on a charge.

Mr Henry got to know Paul through the welfare officer at the local gaol, and thus he came to the centre after his third release from prison. Work was found for him, and, a married man, whose wife had stood by him lived at home.

One night a serious theft took place in a neighbouring store, and was brought to the attention of the CID who very naturally recognized the kind of job Paul used to do. Knowing he was out of prison again enquiries were made as to his whereabouts on the night in question. In the course of his duties, an officer of the CID called at No. 6 Willowbrook Street, where Paul lived. Police, even in plain clothes, are easily recognized in neighbourhoods like Willowbrook Street, where many a household has amongst its numbers those who have been in trouble. The whole district were shortly aware that a visit of enquiry had been made.

'Hello! What's Paul been up to?'

'Saw the bleeders at the house last night.'

Remarks were made, and the children came home from school full of the fact that other children had told them their Dad was in trouble.

Next morning Mrs Paul came to see Mr Henry to tell him of her difficulty. 'And he didn't do it, Sir, I know he didn't. He's really trying to go straight now you've got hold of him,' she said.

This is something that often happens, and it makes life very difficult for the families of old lags. If the town has a centre, it is possible for the police to check with a man like Mr Henry first, finding out if Paul, and others like him, were in the centre during the hours that the offence took place, and so sometimes a visit to the home can be avoided.

This is one of the things that is most frustrating to men who are trying to go straight. They feel resentful that the police keep a check on them and are totally unable, at first, to see why it must be done; but a great deal of help can be given if there is a place they regularly visit and responsible people who know them. In time they can earn back a good character and such incidents become rare. Always, however, the possibility exists.

Outside people know little of the frustration consequent upon enquiries by the police, yet those enquiries must be made in the interests of all, so that crimes are detected.

Men who are honest and have given up their old ways learn to accept such humiliating experiences as part of the price they must pay for their former life—some even derive some satisfaction from their ability to prove their innocence—but to the majority there comes a feeling of hopelessness.

'What's the good of trying? They never give you a chance.'

It is only fair to say that most members of the CID, whilst fulfilling their duties, manage to do so in such a way that the least possible harm is done to innocent people. There is all the difference between an officer who takes the trouble to make enquiries in a reasonable way, and one who rudely bangs on doors—causing all the neighbours to look out of their windows. A housewife can refuse admittance to the police unless they have a search warrant, but this means arguing on the doorstep with the usual interested audience, so few avail themselves of this right.

Jack's wife had suffered several times in this way, and on a day near Christmas the CID had occasion to call at the house in the course of their enquiries when Mrs Jack was entertaining some friends. In came the police, following up a report of stolen radios from an area in the city where Jack had been seen earlier in the day.

Forced by fear of neighbours to bring them into her home, loud voices soon betrayed to the occupants of the back room that the police were there.

One CID officer noted a new radio set in the corner, and without allowing Mrs Jack to explain he picked it up, intending to take it back to the station. The set was newly bought by Jack's wife, out of her own earnings for the family's Christmas present, and was honestly come by. Naturally Mrs Jack seized hold of the set and a struggle ensued in which the new set was damaged and the family thus deprived of their Christmas pleasure.

These things happen. It is one of the results of a criminal past that they can occur.

Had Jack been a member of the centre it is not hard to see that Mrs Jack would have hurried round there for help and sympathy, for which of us would not have turned to friends for comfort in a similar situation?

Left alone, people become hopeless and so often they feel it is no good making any effort to go straight for even when they try they are still hounded because of past misdeeds. Why then should they try? Why not just drift along in the old way? After all, they had their fun in the old bad days, and sometimes they had money to enjoy themselves.

Most people can remember vividly happenings—perhaps in school days—when something unfair occurred. Some occasion when they were blamed for what others had done. How sore they felt! How angry, and how ready they were to hit back. Is it any wonder then that many an ex-prisoner is assisted down the path back to crime by such incidents?

Checks by the police cannot be avoided, but it can be done in a kindly way, and people who are concerned with after-care do well to remember the very real need to discuss the possibility of police investigation with prisoners.

If ex-prisoners are wise they try to spend their leisure time in places where they are known, or in company with people who can vouch for them—particularly at first. Probation officers dealing with after-care are sometimes consulted by the police as to the whereabouts of certain men at stated times, and their knowledge of a man's movements on specified evenings has sometimes saved an enquiry being made at the home.

This suspicion of old lags is by no means confined to the police.

Mary was a young girl in her twenties, whose record showed that she had previously served a borstal sentence after many teen-age years of petty thieving. She had been going straight for three years and was working as a domestic servant in a hospital at the time in question. One day a watch belonging to one of the nurses, and carelessly left in a cloakroom, was missing, so that a search had to be made.

Matron knew of Mary's history—so—as most people would have done in her place—she sent for Mary and questioned her closely. Mary denied ever having seen the watch, which she had not taken, but her record was against her, in spite of the three years' good conduct. Matron felt it her duty to mention Mary's record to others in the hospital in view of the loss of the watch, and it was not long before suspicion focused on her.

Remarks were made in her hearing about the dangers of employing girls with known records of dishonesty, by a few thoughtless people, and every time Mary saw anyone talking in whispers she felt that it was about her. Naturally she ran away.

Unable to get other employment without references, Mary took up her old life of thieving and was later caught and sentenced.

In prison again, with the good years all thrown away, Mary was very bitter. The watch had been found after a few days, where it had fallen into a crack behind the wash basin, and had she stayed her name would have been cleared. It is easy to see how this happened, because almost everyone would have suspected a girl with a known record, should anything be missing, and had Mary been sensible enough to stay, knowing that she was innocent, her character would have been cleared. So often people like Mary take the first opportunity of running away if they sense trouble, and people doing after-care know this only too well.

How truly it has been said by many, that a prisoner's sentence begins when he leaves prison!

These problems, and many more, beset the path of any who try to make a new life for themselves on release.

Difficulties are inevitable, but perhaps if people understood at least a little about them things might be different.

This book can only present a brief picture of the difficulties surrounding a fresh start in life in which outside people play so great a part, whether they know about it or not. Their attitude to such handicapped people can either help or hinder.

It is often the duty of after-care helpers to speak to employers about work for ex-prisoners, and they have met great help and encouragement from many splendid people who are willing and ready to make opportunities. One man recently said 'I have three ex-prisoners in my employment, all of whom have been with me more than a year now. They are splendid men and have given me no trouble in the factory. Their work is good and they have kept up high standards. I am convinced that what is needed is opportunity.' These three men are certainly fortunate, and they all feel they can consult this very fine employer when difficulties arise. Others are less fortunate.

Recently an attempt was made to get an opening for a man in a very large firm where one of the Directors said 'Well, you put me in a bit of a difficulty. You see, we once had someone here who turned out to be an ex-prisoner, and we had to get rid of him. No, I am afraid you must leave us out—sorry, but there it is. The employment situation is not too good and we feel we must study those

men who have always lead honest lives, it wouldn't be
fair to them to take anyone on of doubtful character.'

One can sympathise with this point of view, and many
will feel that the man was right, but the fact remains that
if it were not for the first employer and men like him
there would be far more people in prison than there are
today.

Again, tribute must be paid to all those who have taken
on men and women with records and given them the
chance to make good. It has meant so much to them, and
even if they fail again, it often turns out that they have
not failed the employer who befriended them.

Alf is in prison now. He only worked for two weeks in
a firm in a city when he stole from a car and was caught
and re-sentenced. He has now learned his lesson and will
probably make it next time he is free, but the thing that
has made so great an impression on Alf is that this
particular employer sent a message to him in prison saying
that he was prepared to give him another chance on his
release. 'Alf worked all right for me, and I always believe
in taking people as I find them.'

Alf, who had been rejected all his life by family and
so-called friends as soon as he failed to measure up to
their standards, has now found an employer who will
stand by him even though he has once been let down.
There has been a change in Alf through the months of
his imprisonment and it is likely that next time it will be
different.

Many people with little knowledge of the difficulties
such men have to face have probably added to the general
frustration and hopelessness through no fault of their own,
nor any deliberate unkindness, but through lack of
human understanding.

Another difficulty for the man released from prison is
his relationship with members of the opposite sex.

Many men and women suffer a great deal during their imprisonment from worries and frustrations consequent upon their segregation. So far, although greater knowledge is overcoming the old inhibitions about sex which older generations inherit from former days, this is limited very largely to the better educated men and women of whom fewer exist amongst prisoners.

Pornographic literature and ribald jokes are passed about which provoke sexual stimulation, but a real knowledge of the proper functions and emotions of the human being are rarely known. Untold worry could be avoided if medical staff could make clear the fact that no ultimate harm to sexual powers comes from long periods of abstention from normal relationships.

The result of endless secret worry often means that men on release are over-anxious to prove to themselves that all is well with them, so that often early sexual relationships are formed which lead to involvement and difficulty.

Again, there is the immaturity of the average prisoner after a long sentence, already referred to in an earlier chapter. This causes many a middle-aged man to seek out young girls more suitable to their emotional than their physical age. If things go well with the man after release, he very naturally wants to settle down in a home of his own and longs for someone to share his life. His background is often one without moral values, and chastity has little meaning for him. Probably he has already sampled various illicit relationships but sooner or later he wants to make a more permanent one. Knowing nothing of the deep contentment of complete trust and confidence in another, he sees a girl, wants her, and takes her as soon as he can. He must have everything at once. He rarely gives himself time to get to know the girl, or find out whether she has the same interests and is likely to make a good companion; he begins a complete sexual relationship only too often to find out that it does not satisfy him for long.

The tragedy of an insecure background means to many that the present is everything—there may be no future.

Mr Henry, in his work at the centre, will meet men like Steve. He came out of prison at the age of fifty, and with help began an honest job for the first time in his life. Having no family connections he was lonely, but for some weeks he found friends and company for the evenings. After three months he met a girl of twenty-five who attracted him, and in less than a week the two had set up home together in Steve's lodgings. Nothing was known of Margaret at that time, but it later transpired that she was living apart from her husband and child, whom she had left. Steve was 'in love' as a lad in his teens falls for a girl. Margaret was his girl and she must have everything. Steve was earning good money, and had been encouraged to save, but now all good intentions had gone. Every penny he could raise went on Margaret, who gladly accepted gifts of clothes and jewellery. The job Steve was doing did not provide sufficient for such lavish expenditure, and it soon became known that he was back on the old game—making money for Margaret who was herself unreliable and out for what she could get.

It is easy to see how this can happen, and Steve is now back inside paying in another four years of prison for his impetuous and irresponsible behaviour over Margaret.

The relationship between two immature people, both with a background of insecurity, makes the work of those trying to do after-care most difficult. Neither the man nor the woman can really trust each other, although this is never admitted. Each knows that the other will tell lies and cheat if occasion demands, and therefore they must keep a constant watch upon the other. Should either be late for an appointment, the worst is anticipated, and often a crime of violence caused by jealousy is the outcome of the suspicion which is so much a part of the make up of a criminal.

It is too late to intervene when such relationships are made, but perhaps something can be done in group therapy by frank discussion amongst men in prison with the responsible leadership of a good trained officer or welfare worker.

This is a side of after-care which has been sadly neglected until recently, and even now is only beginning to be recognized.

Men returning to their wives after imprisonment have other problems, and much help can be given before release if discussion can be arranged and an opportunity provided for frank exchange of views with wise counsellors. Such subjects should not be allowed to remain as guilty and embarrassing secrets to men who never had the trained and experienced help of wise and balanced people, for they lead to inevitable trouble after release.

Changes are on the way, and new means of rehabilitating ex-prisoners will be devised. None can be successful unless all those outside the prison can be a little more tolerant, a little kinder and more ready to forgive.

The prodigal son was welcomed back after his loose-living brought him to a state in which he recognized himself for what he was. Alone, he could never had returned to be an accepted member of his family. Many people side with the elder brother whose righteous indignation had blinded him to the truth. The father had understood and seen, even in this wayward youth, a possibility which his brother would not admit.

It would have been interesting if the story had gone on.

Did the prodigal change his way of life because of his father's welcoming love? Or did he return to his old ways after a period of comfort at home?

It will never be known, but although some defend the attitude of the elder brother no one really likes him, nor is it imagined that the prodigal would willingly have stayed at home if the father had not been there.

The way of the elder brother has been tried again and again, and so far this has not proved a satisfactory way of dealing with problem people.

The prisons are still full, men and women once sentenced continue to return to crime, and people suffer from their misdeeds.

Perhaps Mr Henry is right?

Perhaps there will be other 'Mr Henry's' in the future and centres where men and women can seek friendship and support in their hard return to a place in society.

People of good will can do a great deal to assist the after-care services. Employers can be prepared to consider providing opportunities, as many do already, but what of work-mates who suddenly discover that one of their gang has a record? Acceptance, or the cold shoulder? This may be the turning point in the ex-prisoner's life.

It is hard for many ordinary people to feel safe and happy about welcoming an old lag, because of the very natural fear that exists in everyone about the unknown, particularly the unknown criminal. No one would willingly push a man back into crime, but very naturally people feel unable to extend the ordinary courtesies of friendship and trust to one who is known to have consorted with other criminals about whom little is known and much is feared.

In future perhaps prisons and the life within will be less of a closed book. People knowing more about the treatment of offenders may be able to say 'Here is a man who was guilty, but has since had many opportunities for reform and rehabilitation. He is no longer a criminal, but has earned the right to a fresh start in life because he has been in prison where he has been taught a new way. He has learned to work, and has been taught a trade. It is now in his interests and the interest of us all that he should be given another chance.'

This may seem a far-off ideal, but unless the whole conception of prison can be changed, and the emphasis placed on rehabilitation from the moment a man walks down the steps from the dock, there will continue to be thousands of anti-social men and women coming back to normal life, resentful, suspicious and unable to adapt themselves to outside conditions.

The punishment of a prison sentence is the deprivation of liberty, and should never be the treatment of the individual prisoner. It has been achieved in the treatment of juvenile offenders who are sent to Approved Schools, so why not for older men and women?

Reforms in prison administration go on, though limited by financial resources. New recruits to the prison service are learning how much depends on them in their daily contact with handicapped people, but this change in the whole concept of prison will be of no avail unless people outside also reorientate their thoughts and see the ex-prisoner as a man needing help and encouragement at the start of a new life.

THE END

For Product Safety Concerns and Information please contact our EU
representative GPSR@taylorandfrancis.com
Taylor & Francis Verlag GmbH, Kaufingerstraße 24, 80331 München, Germany